ROBERT ALTMAN'S *NASHVILLE*

OUT OF THE ARCHIVES

SERIES EDITORS:
MATTHEW SOLOMON AND PHILIP HALLMAN

Robert Altman's Nashville:
An Archival Exploration
Justin Wyatt

Alan Rudolph's Trouble in Mind:
Tampering with Myths
Caryl Flinn

For information about the series and a complete list of titles see
https://press.umich.edu/Series/O/Out-of-the-Archives

Robert Altman's *Nashville*

AN ARCHIVAL EXPLORATION

Justin Wyatt

University of Michigan Press
Ann Arbor

Published in the United States of America by the
University of Michigan Press
First published February 2026

A CIP catalog record for this book is available from the British Library.

Library of Congress Cataloging-in-Publication Data

Names: Wyatt, Justin, 1963– author
Title: Robert Altman's Nashville : an archival exploration / Justin Wyatt.
Description: Ann Arbor : University of Michigan Press, 2026. | Series: Out of the archives | Includes bibliographical references (pages 153–156) and index.
Identifiers: LCCN 2025027373 (print) | LCCN 2025027374 (ebook) | ISBN 9780472040124 paperback | ISBN 9780472905478 ebook
Subjects: LCSH: Altman, Robert, 1925-2006—Criticism and interpretation | Nashville (Motion picture)
Classification: LCC PN1997.N332 W93 2026 (print) | LCC PN1997.N332 (ebook) | DDC 791.43/72—dc23/eng/20250626
LC record available at https://lccn.loc.gov/2025027373
LC ebook record available at https://lccn.loc.gov/2025027374

DOI: https://doi.org/10.3998/mpub.12709875

The University of Michigan Press's open access publishing program is made possible thanks to additional funding from the University of Michigan Office of the Provost and the generous support of contributing libraries.

The authorized representative in the EU for product safety and compliance is Easy Access System Europe, Mustamäe tee 50, 10621 Tallinn, Estonia, gpsr.requests@easproject.com

To Nicole for the love and the laughter
and to Thomas for the kindness and support

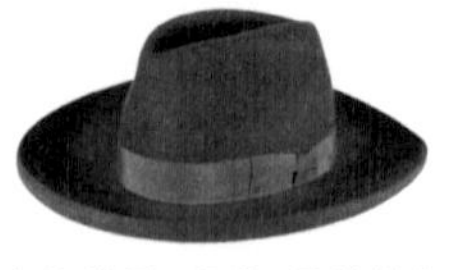

OUT OF THE
ARCHIVES

SERIES EDITORS:
MATTHEW SOLOMON AND PHILIP HALLMAN

Out of the Archives publishes short books that create new knowledge from archival materials in the Screen Arts Mavericks and Makers Collections at the University of Michigan Special Collections Research Center, which document the creative activities of a number of notable independent film and media makers. Books in the series examine subjects and materials that have not received sufficient prior attention, including unsung and unproduced films as well as works that would benefit from reappraisal in light of unexamined archival documents. The series supports researchers' individual trajectories through the archives while encouraging innovative archival configurations, selections, and approaches. A premise of the series is that sustained archival engagements suggest pathways and perspectives that are unavailable through other means and that archival research can generate new paradigms along with new knowledge. The philosophy of the series leverages what can be found in the archives, however fragmentary, incomplete, and idiosyncratic, rather than trying to be comprehensive or definitive.

Each of the individual archives in the Mavericks and Makers Collections is unique and different, like the filmmakers themselves. The respective collections vary in size and box count, although all have been processed and arranged chronologically by project title along the trajectory from pre-production to production through post-production and distribution/exhibition for completed projects. Contents include a wide variety of materials: scripts, correspondence, memos, clippings, notes, ephemera, photographs, along with selected personal items that suggest the ways filmmaking was never a purely professional matter for these individuals who worked independently and/or on the margins of the media industries. For more on the collections, see: https://lib.umich.edu/collections/collecting-areas/special-collections-and-archives/screen-arts-mavericks-and-makers.

Contents

Digital materials related to this title can be found on the Fulcrum platform via the following citable URL: https://doi.org/10.3998/mpub.12709875

Figures

Acknowledgments

I wish to thank the series editors, Matthew Solomon and Phil Hallman, for their support, guidance, and unwavering professionalism throughout this project. Both Matthew and Phil have exercised clear judgment and made smart decisions regarding every aspect of this book, from proposal to final manuscript. At the University of Michigan Press, Haley Winkle and Katie LaPlant have shepherded this book through the press, being helpful, responsive, and caring at every step. Editorial Director Sara Jo Cohen has taken an active interest in this project since its inception. I am particularly indebted to her steadfast backing of the project, even as it has transformed over the years.

This project is centered around artifacts from the Robert Altman Collection in the Screen Arts Mavericks and Makers Collection at the University of Michigan Library. Phil Hallman, Martha O'Hara Conway, and the archive staff worked tirelessly to help me with my research. In addition, I am very happy to acknowledge that the Heid Fellowship from the University of Michigan Library Special Collections facilitated travel to the archives.

I am especially grateful to interview many of Robert Altman's collaborators for this project (and for earlier Altman books). Joan Tewkesbury, Alan Rudolph, Maysie Hoy, Dennis

Hill, Stephen Altman, Dan Perri, and Allan Nicholls offered invaluable background and insights into the making of the film. For an article in *Detour* magazine at the time of *Nashville*'s twenty-fifth anniversary, I was most lucky to interview several actors, including Karen Black, Keith Carradine, Henry Gibson, Scott Glenn, Barbara Harris, Michael Murphy, and Lily Tomlin. At that time, I also spent a wonderful time talking with Robert Altman about *Nashville*, although he clearly was focused on moving forward rather than looking back on his triumphs. *Detour* editor Juan Morales helped greatly with arranging these interviews.

At Paramount Pictures, Andrea Kalas, Jeffrey Christian McCarty, and Dony West shared detailed accounts of experiences of restoring the film through their preservation report, which offered a fascinating snapshot of the team's efforts to locate the assets to create the pristine 4k restoration of *Nashville*. Larry McCallister at Paramount Pictures and Jean Pagliuso supported the project tremendously through granting access to images and artwork for the film.

At the University of Rhode Island, I am thankful to Keith Brown, Cheryl Foster, Scott Kushner, Thomas Stubblefield, and Marybeth Reilly-McGreen for wonderful discussions on *Nashville* and this project. My colleagues and friends in the Departments of Communication Studies, Film/Media and Journalism always offer unfailing good cheer and camaraderie.

I wrote most of this book while on leave from the University of Rhode Island, living in Halifax, Nova Scotia. Knowing no one in that city, I was dependent, even more than usual, on my soulmate, Jeffrey Clarke. Jeff encouraged me, humored me, and always believed in me. He read earlier iterations of this manuscript and offered excellent suggestions for fine-tuning and clarifying arguments and ideas. As we approach our fortieth anniversary, I know that miracles occur on this planet.

Preface

My Road to *Nashville*

Situating the impact of *Nashville* on his life, filmmaker Steve James commented, "I believe that the films we fall in love with, especially when we're younger and falling in love with film, they are films that speak to us because of where we are at in our life."[1] James's sentiment speaks directly to me; *Nashville* was a transformative film for me. My academic interest in *Nashville* cannot be divorced from my personal bond to the film. My hope is that understanding my connection to *Nashville* across time will offer further nuance and context to my analyses in the succeeding chapters.

1974–1975

My very British parents jumped across the pond and decided to live in the Commonwealth. By age ten, I was in Vancouver, in a new school, sporting my English accent. I discovered that, in British Columbia at that time, anyone regardless of age could attend a "Mature" film.[2] With very few friends and a lot of time on my hands, I started going to movies every weekend, solo.

My first Altman film was *California Split* (1974) at the Vogue Theatre in Vancouver. I was then eleven and had arrived very early. I wandered into the theater and watched the last half-hour of the film. After watching the whole film right after, I started to realize something about the film's capacity to create a vivid world; somehow, I was transported by Altman's bright vision of obsessive gamblers, Southern California, and dives. It didn't matter where you started the movie, you would just be immersed in its world. I realized a film's ability to create a world, and for the viewer, the joys of being a voyeur in this world for two hours. This experience was intensified with the film's conclusion: after winning big, Bill (George Segal) tells Charlie (Elliott Gould) that he feels nothing. Bill just goes back to his daily life, and the audience is not rewarded emotionally with a happy ending. I left thinking that this director challenged me as a viewer, a fun activity for a budding cinephile.

The local film critic for *The Vancouver Sun*, Les Wedman, "previewed" *Nashville* in an article in early summer 1975.[3] The description emphasized how the film was not about Nashville but somehow about the whole country. This struck me as fascinating; it was too much for me to comprehend, how a film could be about such an expansive topic. I started to think about everybody having a story, and how most of the time, we have no idea of the unique story of someone right next to us.

The mysteries of *Nashville* were sufficient to keep me invested during the summer. Yes, everybody was talking about *Jaws* (1975), and I certainly was a fan as well. So many around me were chattering about the terrors and adventure of *Jaws*.

The hype was warranted, but after seeing the movie twice, I was ready to move on. Nobody on my block was talking about *Nashville*, which made it even more alluring: I could claim it as "my film," the one I discovered and was an advocate for. I purchased the *Newsweek* issue with *Nashville* on the cover ("Epic of Opry Land") in June.[4] Charles Michener's story gave me background on all the previous Altman films and outlined the director's artistry through his use of performance, sound, and narrative. I used pages of that *Newsweek* issue as a scrapbook for articles on Altman, the film, and the cast. A family vacation in July driving from Vancouver to Los Angeles facilitated another source: I clipped *Nashville* ads from local papers, adding them to my *Newsweek* scrapbook. I was struck by the variety of approaches taken by these newspaper ads. By the Vancouver opening at the Downtown Theatre on August 13, I was fully prepared for the experience.

I attended the opening-day matinee by myself and was surprised by the small audience. After fifty years, I still intensely recall aspects of first watching *Nashville*. The "four-track stereophonic sound," as promised in the ads, made the film more inviting. Conversations, background noise (especially the Walker announcements), and music blasted at me from all directions. The opening titles made me laugh, as I was very familiar with K-Tel record commercials. The fun quotient of the film became an important entry point for me. The snide comments, physical gags, and obvious moments of satire made an impact. Ronee Blakley's music, especially "My Idaho Home" and "Tapedeck in His Tractor," touched me with their imagery of country life, family support, and simple values. The ending, as in *California*

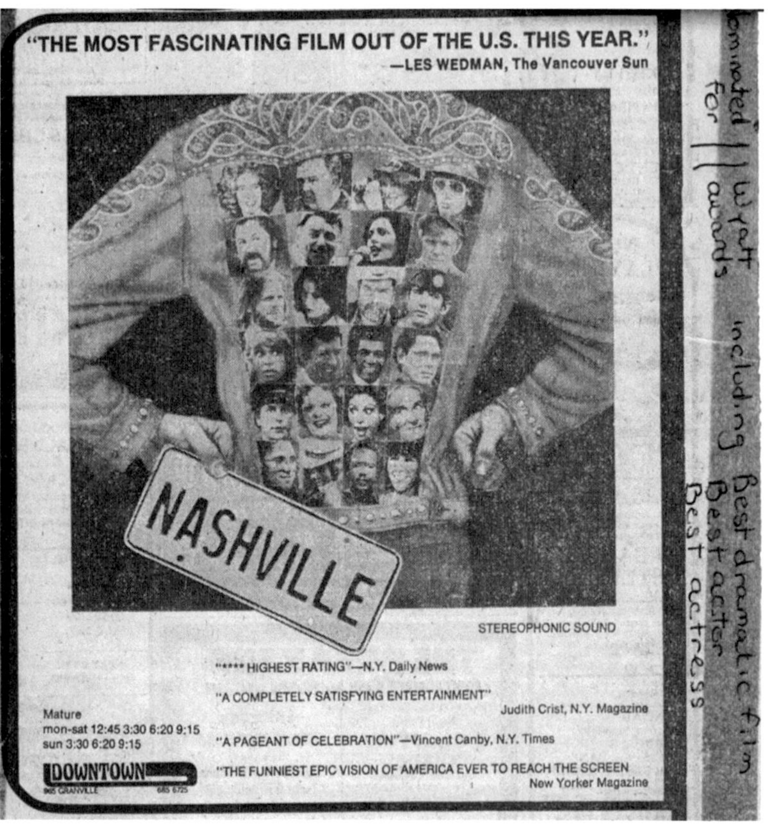

Figure 1: *Nashville* ad, *Vancouver Sun*, with the author's annotation.

Split, was a reminder that life goes on for these characters (and us) after the end of the credits.

Watching *Nashville* three more times that summer, I had a better idea of how a film could be about a country. With its quick pacing, the movement between seemingly unrelated events, and the array of characters, the movie helped me appreciate how characters could crisscross, allowing us to be leading players in our lives but supporting characters or extras in the lives of others. The events unfolding in *Nashville* also created an image of the USA for me: chaotic, ever-changing, racist, fast-paced, adventurous, random, sexist, violent, peculiar, surprising, filled with both good and selfish intentions, and of course, a place where your fortune can change in a heartbeat. Given my own upbringing in England and Canada, the USA through Altman's eyes was intoxicating.

Nashville left Vancouver by early fall. The following summer, in a photography class, I started chatting about how much I loved the film. One of my classmates, Linda Hoy, told me that her sister worked with Robert Altman. Seizing the opportunity, I asked if she could get a letter to Altman for me. Kindly, Linda sent the letter to her sister Maysie, who ensured that Altman received it.[5] I was shocked a few weeks later to get a letter from the director, plus a child-size T-shirt ("*Nashville*: The Damndest Thing You Ever Saw"). This sealed the deal: I was attached to Altman from that point on. Even so, *Nashville* proved to be the high-water mark for me that decade. I really enjoyed *3 Women* (1977), had respect for *Buffalo Bill and The Indians, or Sitting Bull's History Lesson* (1976) and even *Quintet*

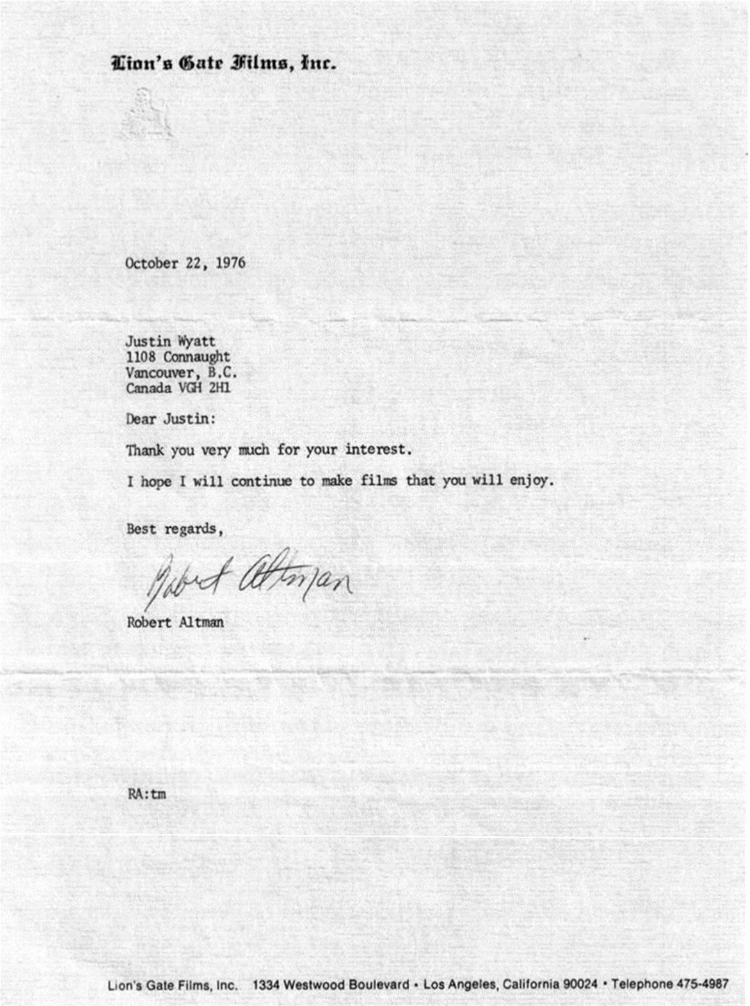

Lion's Gate Films, Inc.

October 22, 1976

Justin Wyatt
1108 Connaught
Vancouver, B.C.
Canada VGH 2H1

Dear Justin:

Thank you very much for your interest.

I hope I will continue to make films that you will enjoy.

Best regards,

Robert Altman

Robert Altman

RA:tm

Lion's Gate Films, Inc. 1334 Westwood Boulevard • Los Angeles, California 90024 • Telephone 475-4987

Figure 2: Letter from Robert Altman to the author, 1976.

(1979), but was more reserved on *A Wedding* (1978) (feeling that Altman's conceit of doubling *Nashville*'s cast from 24 to 48 was unwieldy).

Although I stayed close to home for my undergraduate degree, I ventured to the US for graduate school in film and television studies at UCLA. Over the years, I kept a tie to Altman: writing a journal article on economic imperatives in his career, teaching an Altman course, publishing a seminal Altman text by Robert Self in my book series, and integrating Altman examples into lectures on film history and the New Hollywood. In 2000, I wrote a piece on the twenty-fifth anniversary of the film for *Detour* magazine and was able to interview several cast members, along with Altman and Tewkesbury.[6] Altman was cordial but slightly guarded. The actors, however, were more engaged, and elements of their personalities came through: Henry Gibson, gracious and accommodating; Karen Black, clever and teasing; Barbara Harris, self-deprecating and acerbic; Keith Carradine, sweet and compassionate.

2013–2014

Nashville jumped back into my life in a most unusual way. My spouse was undergoing a serious bout of depression that rendered him incapable of working for some time. Being pragmatic, I realized we would need to move from our Los Angeles home, which we could not afford on one salary. If we could move to a less expensive city, it might be possible to continue with just one of us working. This exit plan came to fruition within a few months: I was offered a marketing research position at a cable network in Nashville. The job was comparable to my current one in terms of responsibility and pay. The difference in cost of living between Los Angeles and Nashville and my spouse's openness to the change helped us make the decision, but Altman was on my mind too.

Understanding that the personal and professional situation was stressful, I was looking for a means to cope. Although I could not admit it then, I was indulging in obviously faulty logic (perhaps given my own stress): I thought my connection to Altman's film would make the transition manageable. It was "my" film, and surely this bond would help make for a favorable move. This dubious connection could be taken as sheer optimism, or perhaps more accurately, as magical thinking. Somehow, I hoped that my favorite film would be a talisman, bringing me luck and good energy to get through a thorny time in my life.

Framing the city of Nashville through the lens of a forty-year-old film classic proved to be ill-advised. Naturally, coming from the West Coast and equipped with a battery of marketing (and research) experiences, I expected to be a modern-day Triplette. While Triplette was able to persuade people to meet his own goals, I was largely a failure at this. I recall a one-hour meeting early on with the network president. Only in the last five minutes was I able to address the content of the meeting and get feedback on some projects. I learned soon after that, in Nashville, the 90/10 rule applies: if you are cordial and friendly, 90 percent of the allotted time will be devoted to the social graces, and about 10 percent to business. I was quick to chat with the locals about *Nashville*. Almost without exception, the response was negative (even after four decades!). The quality of the country music was usually offered as the main reason for disliking *Nashville*. After a few months my boss took me aside and advised, "Don't tell people you like *Nashville*. In fact, don't talk about it at all." I realized that I was much more like Opal than Triplette for these folks.

Themes from the film were apparent in daily life, but Altman's film failed to prepare me for the racial divide that still existed in the city. My own experience showed that racial divisions are so entrenched that a soft segregation still exists. Waiting in line for a prescription at a pharmacy, the young blonde attendant peered at me and asked, "How may I help you, sir?" I responded, "Can you please help these ladies first?" The clerk had disregarded the two black women waiting in line ahead of me. Reality outstripped the illusions offered by the film. Life's messiness exceeded even that of the dense social tapestry depicted by Altman. We left Nashville after two years and I returned to academia.

2017–2024

Attending an event for the Screen Arts Mavericks and Makers collection at the University of Michigan, I was fortunate to have lead archivist Phil Hallman share with me a sample of the Robert Altman archives—at my request, boxes from the archival holdings on *Nashville*. The set of boxes before me contained a wealth of information: contracts, agreements, scripts, publicity stills, scrapbooks of reviews and articles, and personal notes to Altman from actors, directors, and studio executives. The wealth of archival information made me think of first principles: what can we learn about the production, distribution, and reception of the film that adds to the scholarship or shines a light on different perspectives on this work? To that end, I began developing this project revisiting *Nashville*, inspired by the Altman archives.

My *Nashville* exploration coincided with a one-year sabbatical in 2023–2024, during which I lived in Canada for the first time in four decades. Reexperiencing the Canadian culture for an extended period, I was surprised at the differences in day-to-day life. Within a month or so, my initial reaction was that Canadians were, to make a broad generalization, reserved, rule-bound, and modest, and they had a deep commitment to diversity that influenced public policy and social interactions. Dissent was possible but mostly contained by the structures and protocols of Canada's social democracy.

At the same moment, following decades of increasing polarization, the USA was split by the Right and the Left, with people also alienated from both parties. Altman's prescience in linking politics and entertainment is demonstrated in stark terms by a right-wing candidate and ex-president who mobilizes reality-show rhetoric and stardom to entertain, enrage, and mollify the masses. The performance, increasingly outrageous, speaks to those who feel that mainstream politics has left them behind. Entertainment is more important than ideology. In the American political landscape of the third decade of this century, Hal Phillip Walker's commitment to "replacement" seems like the paradigm, some people wanting to replace the status quo and traditional political figures even when there is no a viable alternative. The media, always looking for the best hook, seizes on the divisions at every turn, filling every day with high drama.

Viewed from the distance of another country, *Nashville* gave me hope for the future of the country and a roadmap for navigating it as well. As Kurt Vonnegut noted at the time of *Nashville*'s release, "I have often hoped that the arts could be wonderfully useful in times of trouble. I have seen few examples of that. *Nashville*, however, fulfills my dream. It is a spiritual inventory of America, splendidly frank and honest."[7] *Nashville*'s insights are applicable just as much, if not more, to America in the twenty-first century.

The necessity of expressing yourself and struggling for meaning in *Nashville* spoke strongly to me in our charged political and social time. Now I see that the USA depends on the diversity of voices; if you choose to mute yourself for whatever reason, then you are not fully invested in the project of moving the country forward. *Nashville*, of course, is centered on singing and musical expression. Notice the times that the film foregrounds singing even outside of the professional context: the different choirs on Sunday morning, Linnea with her deaf children singing and signing at home, the Opry hosts with the Goo Goo Candy Clusters jingle, and Sueleen's impromptu serenade to the Tricycle Man at the airport coffee shop.

People in *Nashville* are forever trying to connect through music and other means, but Altman illustrates that another facet of the USA is the difficulty of effective communication. Misread cues, muffled conversations, and words said in the background that are unheard by most people—all are evident throughout the film. Expression is fundamental to the USA, yet often we either are incapable of reaching others or our meaning is unclear. Consequently, my other lesson from the film is that this desire to have an impact in life is an ongoing battle. *Nashville* tells us that in this country, the ability to define ourselves or, more accurately, to redefine ourselves helps to create meaning.

Nashville's finale reminded me of the threat of sudden violence in the USA, which can reorder society and shatter lives in an instant. Since the film's release this tragic element in American life has only grown, as we see in the prevalence of drive-by shootings, racially and religiously motivated violence, and a steady stream of school shootings. Albuquerque's anthem "It Don't Worry Me," a dismissal of the brutal violence and a testament to American resilience, became a call to action for me to start again in the USA, no matter what was happening in the political, social, or cultural background.

I started to see *Nashville* not as an object for study or aesthetic appreciation, but rather as a way for me to engage with the USA when I was living in a different country for the first time in four decades. The lessons of the film from the mid-1970s were wholly applicable almost fifty years later. Was this because the conflicts and contradictions in the country at that time were never resolved? Were the social issues in *Nashville* systemic to the USA? My focus was to find a way to move forward, personally and professionally, at a time when the USA was badly fractured. *Nashville* reminded me that this is the American objective, and everyone in the country is attempting to make progress despite innumerable setbacks and restarts.

By returning to *Nashville* for a research project, I had reactivated the film as a personal framework for living in the USA. The power of the film to serve this function derived from its imprinting on me at such a tender age. Altman had given me a present, albeit one that contained all the delights and demons that are part of living in this messy and vibrant country.

Thomas Merton captured the essence of the art/audience relationship with his observation that "Art enables us to find ourselves and lose ourselves at the same time." Through *Nashville* I have been losing and finding myself for a lifetime. I hope this continues until the lights are turned out. In *Nashville* terms, I began my journey as Linnea's son Jimmy and have ended up as Mr. Green. Altman's work of art has offered meaning and insight to each of the characters I have identified with, depending on who I was at the time and what I needed from the film. Even after all these decades, I still discover images, sounds, and marginal actions that continue to inform my appreciation for Altman's film. *Nashville* is a work of art that shaped my life. Without it, I would not have pursued my nascent interest in film analysis and aesthetics, nor have opened myself to the capabilities of film as a medium and ventured to the USA for grad school and the rest of my life.

CHAPTER 1

The Lure of *Nashville*

Nashville is a beguiling work of art: its fascination comes from director Robert Altman's ability to blend small, quotidian moments, large scenes of spectacle, and disturbing and sharply observed insights into American life. A snapshot of American society firmly rooted in a specific time and place, the film presents a compelling landscape of American dreams, failures, and lies.

Deceptively simple, *Nashville*'s intricate screenplay is anchored by a tight structure juxtaposing twenty-four characters in the city of Nashville across five days. A main connecting thread is the packaging of a political rally for the fictional presidential candidate Hal Phillip Walker. During the film, Walker's advance man John Triplette (Michael Murphy) sets the celebrity lineup for the rally, including leading country stars Barbara Jean (Ronee Blakley), Haven Hamilton (Henry Gibson), and folk-rock trio Tom, Bill, and Mary (Keith Carradine, Allan Nicholls, and Cristina Raines). Other country stars, such as Tommy Brown (Timothy Brown) and Barbara Jean's fill-in Connie White (Karen Black), along with those who are seeking country music fame and fortune, waitress Sueleen (Gwen Welles) and hillbilly wife Albuquerque (Barbara Harris), add to the music scene. Those supporting the country stars professionally and personally appear throughout: manager Barnett (Allen Garfield), lawyer Del Reese (Ned Beatty), Del's wife Linnea (Lily Tomlin), bar owner and Haven Hamilton mistress Lady Pearl (Barbara Baxley), business manager Bud Hamilton (Dave Peel), driver Norman (David Arkin), Pvt. Kelly (Scott Glenn), and purported BBC journalist Opal (Geraldine Chaplin).

Other characters are included simply by being present in Nashville as either residents or visitors: "Tricycle Man" (Jeff Goldblum), senior citizen Mr. Green (Keenan Wynn) and his groupie niece Martha / L.A. Joan (Shelley Duvall), Albuquerque's redneck husband Star (Bert Remsen), cook Wade (Robert Doqui), and the enigmatic young traveler Kenny Fraiser (David Hayward). Most people come together in communal spaces such as the airport, the freeway, churches, and the final political rally. Altman blends characters into crowds like the Grand Ole Opry audience so that viewers appreciate how the different characters fit into the social world of the city. The film climaxes with Kenny's attempted assassination of singer Barbara Jean at the rally. In the ensuing chaos, Albuquerque is handed the mic and she leads the crowd in singing "It Don't Worry Me," a hymn of either resilience or active disregard for the violent tragedy. Perhaps Altman believes that for viewers both meanings can be present simultaneously. This assassination is eerily prescient of John Lennon's murder, five years after the film's release. *Nashville* is, by turns, heartbreaking, farcical, and dramatic.

At once a satire on country music, an unvarnished look

at American life, and a cutting examination of our obsession with fame and celebrity, Altman's film combined midlevel stars (Karen Black, Henry Gibson, Geraldine Chaplin) with members of the director's unofficial repertory company (Shelley Duvall, Michael Murphy, and Bert Remsen, among others) and the Oscar-nominated debuts of singer Ronee Blakley and *Laugh-In* star Lily Tomlin. Although the public response was only fair, the critical reaction was generally very positive. The film garnered an impressive eleven Golden Globe nominations, although it won just Best Song (Keith Carradine's "I'm Easy"). The wide critical acclaim also helped *Nashville* land five Academy Award nominations including Best Picture and Best Director. Ultimately, *Nashville*, apart from Best Song, was ignored by the Academy in favor of a sweep for *One Flew Over the Cuckoo's Nest* (1975).

Robert Altman and the New Hollywood

Nashville appears in 1975 at the zenith of the New Hollywood period of filmmaking. This era developed from a specific set of economic and social circumstances in the wake of the demise of the Hollywood studio system. Set against a period of expensive flops, lack of connection with the moviegoing public, and significant social and political change, the Hollywood studios of the late 1960s searched for ways to become more relevant to their audience. As David Cook describes the situation, the damaging commercial aspects led to an industry-wide recession: "The recession of 1969 had produced more than $200 million in losses: left MGM, Warner Bros., and United Artists under new management; and brought Universal and Columbia close to liquidation."[1] With legacy Hollywood failing to meet the needs of the audience, Hollywood began to consider some alternatives, aesthetically and industrially. To that end, the period of the late 1960s through the mid-1970s ushered in films that were more creative in both form and content, often guided by the vision of a Hollywood auteur. Directors such as Martin Scorsese, Brian DePalma, Arthur Penn, Francis Coppola, Bob Rafelson, Hal Ashby, and Robert Altman were among those responsible for these challenging films, which treated the audience as adults, often presenting more questions than answers in their films. With the demise of the Production Code and the institution of the Motion Picture Association of America Ratings System, films of this period could explore more adult subject matter and social concerns. The New Hollywood eventually succumbed to more market-oriented films with simple premises and an emphasis on franchise action spectacles, a trend that has continued for decades.[2]

After a lengthy career directing episodic television, Altman directed two features: the space exploration drama *Countdown* (1967) and the psychological thriller *That Cold Day in the Park* (1969). Neither made a significant impact with critics or the public. But with his Korean War–era comedy *M*A*S*H* (1970), Altman's place in the New Hollywood was set. Telling of the exploits in the operating theater and beyond of surgeons Hawkeye (Donald Sutherland) and Trapper John (Elliott Gould), the film mixed anarchy, social critique, broad satire, and chillingly realistic surgery scenes. It tapped into the countercultural sentiment toward the Vietnam War and became both a critical and commercial hit. In the five years between *M*A*S*H* and *Nashville*, a prolific Altman directed six features. Whether through character, visual style, or genre investigation, each film created a vivid environment for the viewer: a comical take on the Houston Astrodome for a man hoping to fly in *Brewster McCloud* (1970); the development of a frontier Pacific Northwest town in *McCabe & Mrs. Miller* (1971); the isolated Irish mansion harboring a splintered mind in *Images* (1972); detective Phillip Marlowe placed in present-day Los Angeles in *The Long Goodbye* (1973); the seedy fringe gambling world of *California Split*; and the recreation of an impoverished 1930s Mississippi in *Thieves Like Us* (1974). The incredible diversity of places, stories, and characters illustrates Altman's fertile and creative mind and his ability to transport viewers to fully realized worlds, both unexpected and uncharted.

During this period, other aesthetic and production elements began to be associated with Altman. He populated his films with vivid, distinctive, idiosyncratic characters. These characters were built through performances by a collection of actors, from established stars to veteran supporting players and nonactors; casting was crucial to Altman's aesthetic. The performances were often enhanced by naturalistic behavior and off-the-cuff dialogue, making the viewer a fly on the wall for much of the action. This realism in design was bolstered by overlapping soundtracks, with actors speaking at the same time against background sound. For Altman this tactic simply mirrored the way that people spoke in everyday life.

The net impact of Altman's brand was to confound viewer

expectations of character, narrative, and genre. Audiences failed to connect with most of these films; in fact, of the six films between *M*A*S*H* and *Nashville*, only one broke even financially. Except for *Brewster McCloud*, the other films were embraced by critics, with Pauline Kael a particular champion for Altman in this period. *Nashville* culminated the experiments in sound, narrative, and structure that Altman had been pioneering in the years after his success with *M*A*S*H*.

Nashville: Innovative Design

Compositionally, *Nashville*'s inventiveness comes from Altman creating a realistic film through genre, observational filming, and sound design that nevertheless is guided strongly by an overriding vision. Consequently, the viewer experiences a work of art firmly anchored in the real world. Through establishing the film's realism, Altman creates a space for the viewer to become part of the film. This immersion flirts with an emotional connection to the characters, although ultimately *Nashville* is more invested in engaging viewers intellectually. As screenwriter Joan Tewkesbury explains it, the viewer becomes part of the film's structure: *Nashville*, based around twenty-four characters, lets the viewer become the twenty-fifth.[3]

Nashville shifts, time and again, between different aesthetic modes and narrative categories. As a result, the film can be daunting for first-time viewers. This is a film that benefits from multiple viewings, with nuances of story, character, and drama becoming clearer over time. In terms of genre, the film borrows from both the musical and the documentary, although its design fits neither mode perfectly. Altman encouraged the actors playing the country singers to write their own songs. Impressively, *Nashville* has more than 100 minutes of music, but much of this is either heard behind dialogue or presented so we hear only a snippet of the song. Nevertheless, following the musical genre, song is used in *Nashville* to comment on the action and to move the story forward. Haven Hamilton's patriotism ("200 Years"), resilience ("Keep A-Goin'"), and family values ("For the Sake of the Children") are built through his songs. Similarly, Barbara Jean's devotion to family and her country comes through clearly with songs like "My Idaho Home," "Tapedeck in His Tractor," and "Dues." *Nashville* is a backstage musical in that the musical numbers and cues are motivated within the film's world. In this way, *Nashville* is rooted in realism and faithful to the everyday world built carefully during the film.

Altman borrows aspects of the documentary film, or, more precisely, a kind of observational cinema in building *Nashville*. The film is shot with minimum artifice: the camera records events that seemingly appear to be happening spontaneously. Scenes that center on actors talking will also include other actors, often mute, on the periphery of the action. Accordingly, the cast is sewn into the larger landscape of Nashville. Betraying his television background, Altman and cinematographer Paul Lohmann use the zoom shot to bring attention to specifics within a scene. As Mark Minett notes, this device is practical in nature; the zoom allows the filmmaker to reveal details while shooting in real-world settings not open to more elaborate dolly shots. Shot on location and using city residents in many crowd scenes, from the airport arrival of Barbara Jean to the concert scenes at the Grand Ole Opry, Parthenon, and Opry Belle, the film benefits greatly from the local Nashville residents filling the frame. This is particularly true in the film's finale. After Barbara Jean's assassination, Albuquerque leads the crowd in singing "It Don't Worry Me." Altman concludes with many shots of individuals singing in the crowd, including little children clapping along to the song. When matched with shots of police walking through the audience, viewers understand how Altman is indicting American society for complacence: people happily sing, forgetting the violence, while being monitored by authorities. Without the observational aesthetic, these points could not be made effectively by the director.

The realist and observational perspectives are enhanced greatly by Altman's sound design for the film. Altman had been experimenting with sound significantly in the early 1970s. Instead of relying on a boom mike to catch sound in a scene, Altman wired each person in the scene for sound. This permitted up to eight separate tracks, including one to catch background noise.[4] The system allowed for multiple conversations simultaneously and for freedom of movement. As Jay Beck comments on Altman's use of sound, "While overlapping dialogue was not new to Hollywood filmmaking, Altman revitalized the technique in his films by multiplying the number of speaking voices and divorcing them from their spatial relationship to the camera and the frame."[5] The system, allowing for multiple conversations, let Altman dial up some soundtracks and dial down others in the sound mix.

Even a simple scene at an airport diner becomes more realistic through the sound design. Altman cuts between a magic trick with the saltshaker done by the Tricycle Man (Jeff Goldblum) while Mr. Green is giving his order to Sueleen. The trick continues as Mr. Green tells the patron beside him about his wife's illness. The effect is unusual because you often can't see on screen the actors talking. Altman expands the possibility for understanding the environment, and especially the ways through which we can realize a more complete aural and visual sense of the space. One consequence of the sound design in *Nashville* is to refigure the viewer's attention: the viewer is constantly called to the periphery of the action, rather than the center. This level of realism is also reflected in the musical scenes. Instead of the typical method using actors lip-synching to a prerecorded track, Altman recorded all of the music live.

Sound serves another function in *Nashville*. The busy soundtrack is used to work against building sentiment for the characters and their situations. This may seem counterintuitive, but it is deliberate on Altman's part. One consequence of this emotional "blunting" is that plotlines that would normally elicit an emotional response fail to do so. Consider the hospital scene where Mr. Green finds out his wife has died. The nurse must repeat the information twice due to his hearing. Immediately after this news, Pvt. Kelly sidles up to Mr. Green, telling him a lengthy story of his mother saving singer Barbara

Jean. Immediately after the story, Altman cuts to Triplette listening to Opal's theory of assassination. Mr. Green has been painted as a sympathetic character dealing with his sick wife and his rude and careless niece. His wife's unexpected passing would seem to be a spot to elicit feelings for the character, but Altman does his best to limit this emotional connection: Pvt. Kelly's detailed story derails the scene, and then Altman cuts to Triplette and Opal laughing as she talks about the "real assassins" in American society. Between Kelly's information and then cutting to laughter, sound is used with the editing to push the viewer away from an emotional reaction. Since the film resists presenting a typical emotional engagement, the viewer is forced to read the film another way. This reading is reinforced by *Nashville* music director Richard Baskin, who describes an unsatisfied audience reaction to the film: "I think people were responding emotionally to what was quite an intellectual film."[6]

Working against the realist aesthetic, Altman also foregrounds several self-conscious narrative devices. These are in line with postclassical Hollywood's adoption of authorial expressivity. Even while constructing the film, Altman wants the viewer to remember that the viewer is, indeed, watching a film. The title credits sequence potently announces this self-conscious tendency. Many title credits are placed inconspicuously against either a simple graphic or an element within the mise-èn-scene, Altman and title designer Dan Perri create opening credits in the hard-sell style of a late-night record commercial of the era. Introducing each actor in the bellowing voice-over, the tone is self-mocking: even a first-time actor

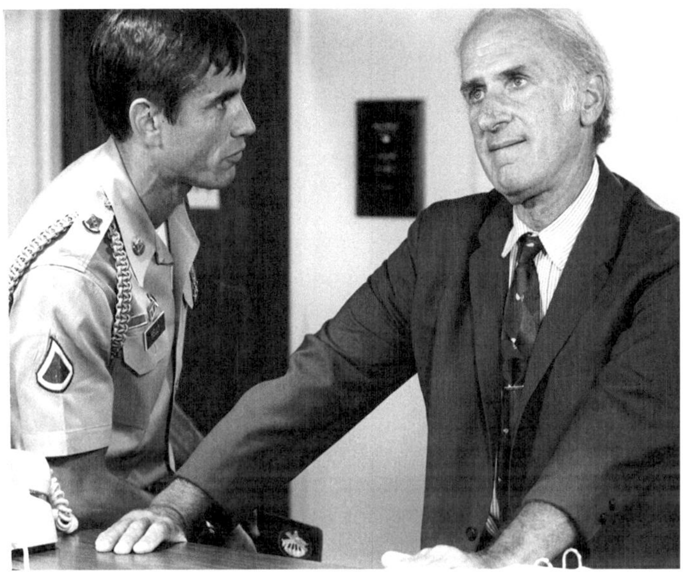

Figure 3: Pvt. Kelly talks to Mr. Green after devastating news.

like Dave Peel is referred to as "the all-time great!" The rushed, bold voiceover is accompanied by two visual elements: a spinning carousel of record albums by the fictional country stars in *Nashville* and the sketch of each actor from *Nashville*'s record album cover. The effect is explosive: the titles sequence calls attention to the commercial construction of the film, teasing the viewer with the high-energy fake sell of the voice-over and visuals. We are reminded that *Nashville* is just as cynical and calculated as the relentless music commercials. Rather than easing the viewer into the film, Altman breaks the cinematic world, and the viewer knows that we are watching a piece of packaged entertainment.

Star cameos in *Nashville* reflect a similar level of self-consciousness. Altman regular Elliott Gould (star of *M*A*S*H*, *The Long Goodbye*, and *California Split*) plays himself, visiting Haven Hamilton's party and interacting with (real-life) press liaison Sue Barton. Julie Christie, from Altman's *McCabe & Mrs. Miller*, also playing herself, is escorted by Barton to meet Haven Hamilton and Connie White at a country-and-western club. Unlike in most mainstream American films, the self-consciousness splinters the film, arguing against an emotional attachment to the characters and their stories.

Realism and self-consciousness push in opposite directions, and this tension creates a film that is an open text. Rather than impose an interpretation on viewers, Altman gives space to allow many different, and at times contradictory, takes on individual scenes, characters, and lines of action. A good example of this strategy is Tom singing "I'm Easy" at the Exit/In club. Tom dedicates the song to "someone special" who may be in the audience. As he sings, the camera finds in the audience three women (L. A. Joan, Mary, and Opal) who had affairs with Tom, and another, Linnea, who is currently being seduced by the Lothario. The song tells of a man who can be manipulated emotionally and sexually by a partner—"easy" to those who love him. The scene can be accepted on the basis of the dramatic stakes: whether Linnea will be wooed by Tom and won over by his singing. Alternately, a comic reading comes from the multiple women present, all of whom think the song could be about them. Finally, the scene could be interpreted as a satirical take on the sexual freedom of that period: all the promiscuity is accompanied by an emotional

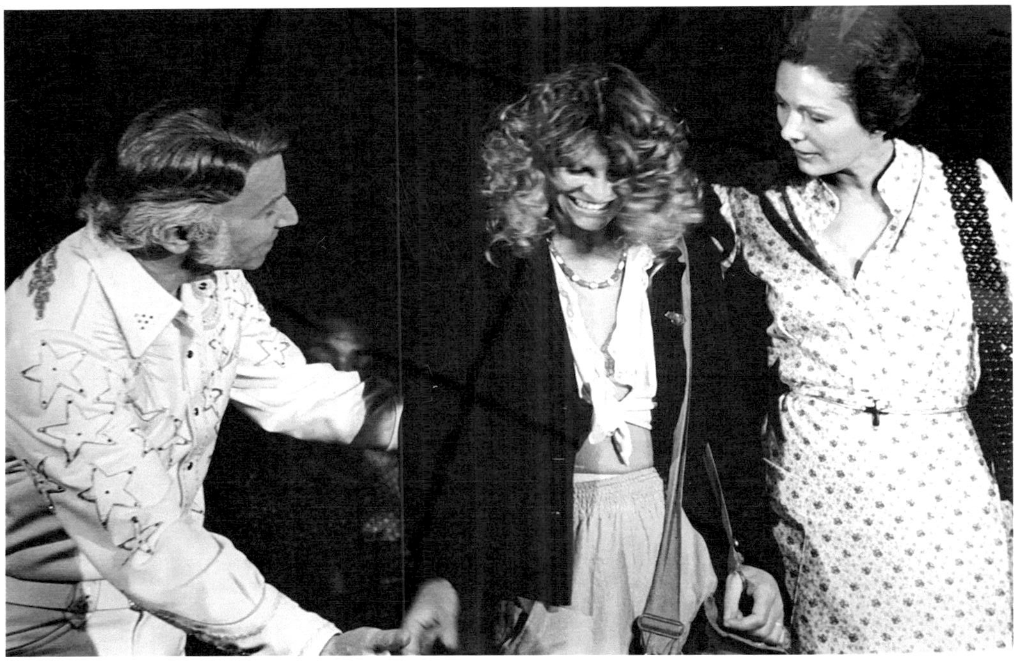

Figure 4: Julie Christie (center) makes a cameo in *Nashville*.

emptiness. The openness of the film accommodates all these readings, and viewers can appreciate more than one interpretation at the same time.

Across the Decades

Since its release, *Nashville*'s place among the most influential works in the New Hollywood has become even more secure. In 1992, the film was added to the National Film Registry, designed to preserve "culturally, historically or aesthetically significant films." For its twenty-fifth anniversary in 2000, Jan Stuart authored *The Nashville Chronicles*, a comprehensive review of *Nashville*'s planning, production, release, and legacy. *Nashville* also places on the British Film Institute (BFI) 100 Greatest Films list voted by critics and directors.

Issued on DVD by Paramount in 2000, the film received greater visibility in 2013 with a two-disc DVD/Blu-ray set from the Criterion Collection. This release benefited from a 2k digital film restoration. Recognizing the deterioration of the original film elements, Paramount conducted a restoration starting in 2018. The goal was to secure the highest-resolution source material for every frame of the film in 4k. This effort yielded the 4k Blu-ray of *Nashville* from the Paramount Presents series in 2021. The impressive restoration was featured in an Altman retrospective at the BFI and a rerelease to theaters in the United Kingdom.

Over the last half-century, *Nashville* has been the focus of many thoughtful and insightful analyses and explorations. Soon after its release, a flurry of journal articles, interviews, and considerations addressed the movie's unique design and structure (e.g., in the bibliography, consult Connie Byrne and William O. Lopez, Larry Gross, Jane Feuer, Michael Klein, and Sid Levin). Either in chapters or in whole volumes, books analyzing Altman, including his work on *Nashville* and his role in the New Hollywood, started appearing in both academic (e.g., authors such as Robert Self, Robert Kolker, Virginia Wright-Wexman, Gerard Plecki, Robin Wood, Alan Karp, and Helene Keyssar) and trade presses (e.g., Judith Kass, Diane Jacobs, James Monaco, David Sterritt, and David Thompson). In the new century, Stuart's dazzling history of *Nashville* has been accompanied by invaluable works by Mitchell Zuckoff, Adrian Danks, Ryan Gilbey, Chris Horn, and Mark Minett.

This book does not seek to replicate prior scholarship. Rather, I am interested in pursuing critical inquiries inspired by artifacts in the *Nashville* archive. Housed in the University of Michigan Special Collections, the *Nashville* archive was donated by Altman's widow Kathryn Reed Altman in 2008. Ranging from personal correspondence to script drafts and studio publicity, the Altman archive on *Nashville* is extensive.

Chapter by Chapter

This book draws from the archives for a critical and historical inquiry on the film, and at times from Altman's larger body of work. The chapters use archival material for a deep dive into *Nashville* through exploring the social and political landscape, its marketing, and the collaborative process behind the film. Interviews with Altman's collaborators are another inspiration in this project. Rather than fit the archival materials and interviews into a preexisting critical or theoretical framework, the book grew from these inputs as a starting point. In this way, the work is truly a function of the Altman archive and what might be gleaned from it.

Although the press often mischaracterized *Nashville* as being largely improvised by the cast under the guidance of Altman, early versions of the script reveal how critical Joan Tewkesbury's vision was to the structure and development of the film. Through analysis of a late script draft (fourth version, about five months prior to production), interviews with Altman's collaborators, and particularly my own interview with Tewkesbury, in chapter 2 I trace how the screenwriter's contribution was minimized by Altman and largely also within the press. This analysis is not designed to discredit Altman and his creativity. Rather, I am interested in understanding how Altman collaborated with Tewkesbury in both preproduction and during filming. The label of screenwriter is perhaps the largest problem: it fails to encapsulate the intimate working relationship among Tewkesbury, Altman, and the large cast.

Released just before America's bicentennial, Altman's film is widely viewed as an examination of America at that point in time. This can be appreciated even in the first scene of Haven Hamilton cutting the new song "200 Years." Accordingly, the film embodies a whole set of opinions and attitudes on how America functions. Shot in the summer of 1974, the country was reeling from Watergate, the Vietnam war, inflation, the gas crisis, and the struggle for civil rights, among other contingencies. On the civil rights front, *Nashville*'s placement of gender and race speaks to the larger divisions in the country, then and now. Chapter 3 unpacks the political and social ideological strands of *Nashville* using images and documents from the Altman archive.

Altman introduced the political throughline to Tewkesbury's original screenplay by asking author Thomas Hal Phillips to draft a political platform that would be appealing and different from the two-party options. This chapter also examines the Walker political platform and how it has been reflected in various political figures and events over the past five decades. The Altman archive contains background on the fictional candidate, along with explanations of his policies and opinions. As with much political rhetoric, the pronouncements from the Walker van become white noise for most of the people nearby. Using images from the Walker pamphlets and propaganda in the Altman archive, this chapter presents the key elements of the campaign and connects the dots from Walker's platform to politicians, issues, and policies of our time.

As would be expected from a film made five decades ago, the portrayal of race and gender falls behind our current conceptions. Nevertheless, it is worth investigating how these representations are configured and what they mean to the functioning of the film. This presentation also decides who is at the center of the narrative and who is on the periphery. Although *Nashville* has twenty-four characters, there are large discrepancies between the characters in terms of definition and function within the film. The chapter also demonstrates how the American dream may be fitfully alive, but only at the expense of many groups and the personal and professional failures of others.

In chapter 4, I explore how *Nashville* was marketed through advertising, including posters, the trailer, and affiliated media. This investigation is designed to show the difficulties of positioning *Nashville* in the film marketplace and the ways the marketing helped shape the image and public perception of the film. *Nashville* marketing and advertising materials have been gathered from the Altman archive and the Paramount Pictures archive. There is a gulf between the advertising and marketing sponsored by Paramount and that affiliated with Altman. Paramount clearly struggled to express the essence of the film in a two-minute trailer and a print ad. Altman sided with an original artwork by J. William Myers, a Nashville artist. Painted from photos taken by Myers while the film was shooting, the finished artwork is pitched much closer to a cartoon than to a realistic representation of the twenty-four actors. Crucially, though, the artwork succeeds in creating a sense of fun while conveying the relationships between the characters, given the placement, gestures, and expressions of the figures.

The Altman archive includes *Nashville*'s photographic contact sheets, along with stills, publicity shots, and continuity photos. A close examination reveals that several scenes or sequences in these images do not occur in the finished film. Chapter 5 ponders the impact of these omissions: connecting and facilitating transitions between scenes and offering footage that contradicts our understanding of a character. Analysis in this chapter illustrates how the contact sheets can signal different trajectories for characters, storylines, and narrative arcs, enriching our understanding of the film's complete world. A brief coda to this book brings together key themes and issues weaved throughout and suggests a way to conceive of *Nashville*'s value to a contemporary audience.

CHAPTER 2

Collaboration and Visibility

Given his formidable track record for making innovative and challenging films in the 1970s, Robert Altman is often cited as one of the leading directors of this era. The New Hollywood auteurs split into a younger, film-school group (e.g., George Lucas, Francis Coppola, Martin Scorsese, Steven Spielberg) and an older set with prior experience in television, film, or both (e.g., Arthur Penn, Sidney Lumet, Altman). As Maya Montañez Smukler notes in *Liberating Hollywood: Women Directors and the Feminist Reform of 1970s American Cinema*, opportunities for female director were much more limited in this era.[1]

Altman leveraged his power as a New Hollywood auteur to create an image as an iconoclastic, "bad boy" director with contempt for the "suits" in the Hollywood studios. This image was crafted through interviews and publicity associated with his films. An often-overlooked element of Altman's auteurism is his collaboration with members of his creative team. On *Nashville*, Altman credits four primary collaborators: associate producer Scott Bushnell, assistant director Alan Rudolph, production manager Tommy Thompson, and screenwriter Joan Tewkesbury.[2] Bushnell was included for her casting and wardrobe assistance, Rudolph for shooting background scenes and extras, and Thompson for organizing the schedule and logistics of the shoot. Certainly, all helped shape the film, but Tewkesbury's contribution was the most crucial. In this chapter, I explore the collaboration between Joan Tewkesbury and Robert Altman with an eye to understanding how her creative work can be appreciated separate from Altman's auteur branding. I do not seek to diminish the collaboration between the two. The goal is to illuminate Tewkesbury's vision, which has often been overshadowed by commentary on Altman's filmmaking and auteurism.

Building the *Nashville* Screenplay

Tewkesbury's affiliation with Altman began on *McCabe & Mrs. Miller*; she served as script supervisor and played a small role in the film. Altman asked Tewkesbury to write an adapted screenplay of the novel *Thieves Like Us* by Edward Anderson, already a Nicholas Ray film titled *They Live by Night* (1948). Tewkesbury joined Altman for filming on location in Mississippi. The director had disliked a United Artists script, *The Great Southern Amusement Company*, but told the studio executives he would develop a country-and-western script. To that end, during the *Thieves* production, Altman sent Tewkesbury to visit the city of Nashville and to gather information for a screenplay. Accompanied by singer/songwriters Bill and Taffy Danoff, Tewkesbury's initial stay proved to be less than fruitful as she visited a variety of Nashville tourist attractions and historical sites, from a museum featuring Patsy Cline's hairpins to a Bible-printing museum.[3] As Tewkesbury described it, "I got the docent's tour of the museum."[4]

A second trip to Nashville during which Tewkesbury explored by herself in a more free-form manner was much more revealing. Observing that the city was built in a circle, Tewkesbury noticed that you would encounter the same people two or three times during the day. Parts of this visit were borrowed for her screenplay, but, most significantly, she had found the structure for the project. Characters would crisscross in public and private spaces, and an imposing eighteen characters wove their stories through the film. Tewkesbury refers to this structure as a "piece of choreography" performed in very specific atmospheres and locations.[5] Incidents in the film echo Tewkesbury's second visit, including the freeway crash and her visit to Exit/In club. Knowing that Altman favored a communal setting, as in *McCabe & Mrs. Miller*, Tewkesbury populated her script with a landscape of Nashville denizens including a leading country star, a lawyer, a limousine driver, and a short-order cook.

Altman added two essential elements to the mix: the political campaign and the assassination at the end. Knowing that Altman's films often conclude with a death, Tewkesbury originally ended the screenplay with Sueleen committing suicide. Altman shifted a political assassination to the entertainer. Although Kenny signals that he is interested in Hal Phillip Walker (his car back seat is filled with Walker campaign leaflets), the young man changes his target to the country star instead.[6] With the political line added, the number of characters grew from eighteen to twenty-four. As Tewkesbury men-

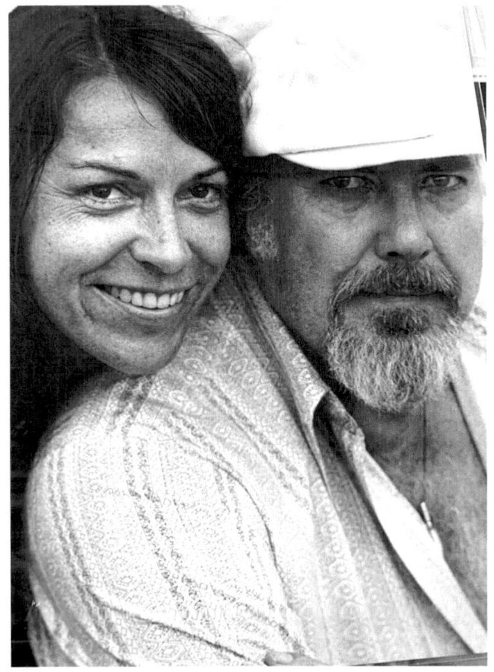

Figure 5: Joan Tewkesbury and Robert Altman.

tioned, these additions also came from Altman simply casting people; the Lady Pearl character, hardly a blip in the original screenplay, became one of the characters once Altman chose Barbara Baxley, who he knew from his television directing career. Tewkesbury kept track of the comings and goings of her characters though a wall chart with the character names on the horizontal axis and the days of the week / time of day on the vertical.[7] She wanted to keep control of where each character would be, with whom, and what they would be doing. The goal was to see each character every day.

Weaving the characters throughout each day, Tewkesbury ended up with a snapshot of the city across eleven days (later trimmed to five by the start of shooting). The initial screenplay was a lengthy 175 pages, partly because the screenwriter wanted the characters and their backgrounds to be specific. Tewkesbury offers a caveat at the start of the screenplay: "This script is long in page count due to passages of detailed description of characters and events, many of which happen simultaneously. Actual dialogue page count is normal script length." Tewkesbury continued to hone the script through several drafts, adding characters at Altman's request and adjusting the throughline to accommodate the assassination. Almost as an affront to Altman's call to action, the writer made the most likable character, young midwestern visitor Kenny (David Hayward), the killer.

As in their previous collaboration, Tewkesbury joined the director for filming on location. Her function on set is covered much less often than anecdotes about the actors "improvising" during the shoot. Tewkesbury served as a consultant, working with the actors as they prepared for their scenes. As she recounts, she would collaborate with the actors if requested: "Actors would come maybe two or three days before they were going to shoot if they had been thinking about something improvisational. And then on the day of shooting, everyone would assemble on the set, wherever it was, and it would be not so much improvisation, but additions or suggestions."[8] Actors could either follow the script or make changes in their dialogue. Three actors received critical and public attention for their contribution: Ronee Blakley for writing Barbara Jean's lengthy breakdown on stage at the Opry Belle, Barbara Baxley's poignant memories for Lady Pearl of the Kennedy brothers and her political commitment to them, and Geraldine Chaplin's detailed and very off-kilter Opal observations on life in Nashville and America. These actors were able to build their characters through these contributions, becoming a larger part of the film.[9]

Keep in mind that Tewkesbury played a role by editing drafted dialogue from each actor and then finessing how these words would be integrated into the scene. Tewkesbury explains that the function of each scene, the setting, and the overall structure would remain intact: "You do very specific locations or places to let actors in. If they came in the front door and go out the back door, what happens in the middle could shift or change. The structure would still support the story everybody wanted to tell."[10] Apart from the extended monologues for Barbara Jean, Opal, and Lady Pearl, the "improvised" dialogue comes through in offhand comments that capture a character or situation vividly. This might be minor, like Allan Nicholls's quip ("Wait a minute. Hal Phillip Walker looks exactly like Connie White") looking at a Walker sticker on a poster at the airport or a line that sums up a character completely, like Karen Black's swipe at Julie Christie ("She can't even comb her hair"), revealing the petty, mean, and superficial nature of Connie White. While some actors (e.g., Barbara Harris, Allen Garfield, Karen Black) were comfortable adding their own lines, others (e.g., Keenan Wynn,

Cristina Raines, Keith Carradine) wanted to stay with Tewkesbury's scripted dialogue. This issue failed to have an impact on those who either had no lines (Jeff Goldblum) or had very limited speaking parts (e.g., Shelley Duvall, Bert Remsen).

Positioning the Screenplay

The collaboration between Tewkesbury and Altman must be filtered through the ways that Altman and others discussed the screenplay during publicity for the film's release. Altman was certainly aware of his status as an auteur, and he cultivated a specific image for himself in the press. On a personal level, Altman often presents himself as an iconoclast devoted to smoking dope, drinking heavily, gambling, and, as reported often over the years, clashing with studio executives. A *Variety* writer summed up Altman at the time of *Nashville*'s release as "unpredictable and artistically self-indulgent."[11] A big personality on set and off, Altman, while beloved by actors, was seen as the master and final decision-maker for all his projects. Lily Tomlin teasingly referred to him as "the benign patriarch."[12]

Publicity began with Pauline Kael's prerelease review of a *Nashville* rough cut. While less than fifteen minutes longer than the completed film, Kael's rapturous account of *Nashville* in the *New Yorker* angered other critics, partly for breaking protocol by reviewing an unfinished film. In Altman's interviews and articles, two themes recur: the actors writing their own songs, and Altman discarding the script so his actors can work freely during production. Barbara Harris recalls Altman telling Bert Remsen to put aside his script: "You can throw that away. You won't need it."[13] Altman characterized his method of working as "I don't even look at a script once we start. A script is like a blueprint."[14] With *Nashville*, Altman told writer Sally Quinn that, by the time shooting starts, "nobody can find a script. Literally."[15]

This axiom serves as a cornerstone for Altman's auteurism: writers/journalists latch onto the idea that Altman can transform the "blueprint" through creative collaboration and contributions from his actors. How this transformation takes place is considered less often in articles dealing with the *Nashville* release. Rather, the term "improvisation," guided by Altman, is invoked as an important part of Altman's talent. This creates misleading and ambiguous statements like the *People* magazine article claiming, "Director Robert Altman hired Blakley as a second choice, made her improvise her lines—and turned her into a star."[16] Improvisation is used as a mysterious surrogate to explain Altman's creativity. Similarly, a *New York Times* article connected to the film's release claims that the actors made up "lines, business and whole scenes of the complex film."[17] The suggestion that the actors created whole scenes works against many other accounts of the film sticking closely to the scenes and structure in Tewkesbury's elaborate screenplay.

Altman fostered the notion that improvisation and ignoring the script were pivotal in his filmmaking. This bolstered his image and collaterally became a marketing ploy for his films, including *Nashville*. Reviewing articles associated with the film, Altman offered conflicting statements on how the improvisation operated. The director claimed in an interview to have written all of Geraldine Chaplin's monologues, but this is contradicted in many other accounts that give credit solely to Chaplin.[18] Certainly, on other occasions, Altman credited the actors and Tewkesbury for adding dialogue to the film.

One consequence of improvisation as an Altman intervention is to diminish the role of the screenwriter in his projects. This tendency was evident several years before *Nashville.* George Litto, the talent agent who packaged the creative elements for *M*A*S*H*, stated, "Bob (Altman) was never one to acknowledge a writer's contribution. The movie was 90 percent Ring Lardner's script, but Bob started saying he improvised the movie. I said, 'Bob, Ring Lardner gave you the best opportunity you had in your life. He's been blacklisted for years. What you're doing is very unfair to him and you ought to stop.'"[19]

Altman's connection to Tewkesbury's *Nashville* script is more conflicted. She has stated that Altman hated the first draft. His longtime collaborators Robert Eggenweiler and Tommy Thompson disagreed with the director, telling Altman that the script was great.[20] Decades later, Tewkesbury shared that Altman wanted to contribute to the screenplay before he could acknowledge its worth; as she explains, "See, he hated it until he could put his two cents in and then it was fine."[21] Tewkesbury incorporated Altman's suggested changes and worked on subsequent drafts. Altman readily acknowledges Tewkesbury's contribution on set, as evidenced in this interview from July 1975:

> [Joan Tewkesbury] was there during the shooting on both *Nashville* and *Thieves* all the time, and she would write scenes, some-

times; sometimes she would talk to actors. She'd say, "Is there anything you would want to give me? Do you want more background on yourself? Do you want me to write a scene for you or do you want to write a scene for yourself?" In other words, she was there as a point of service.[22]

The phrase "point of service" speaks to Altman's restrained view of Tewkesbury's contribution. As she is to be "of service" to the actors in crafting their characters, the writer's own agency is diminished, although Altman's explanation of the many roles played by Tewkesbury on location matches other accounts. Rather than connect Tewkesbury's work on the screenplay over months with her ongoing creative contributions during production, Altman describes her function as transactional, to facilitate the actors' character-building.

Altman's disenfranchisement of the screenwriter can be inferred from several factors. First, Altman attempted to get a writing credit on the film. This move was blocked by an attorney who vouched for Tewkesbury's work.[23] Also, little attempt was made to lobby for Tewkesbury for an Oscar nomination for original screenplay. Tewkesbury believed that Altman wanted to maximize his own chances of being nominated as director and producer: "He was angling for a nomination, and so it was best not to spend too much time talking about the writer. If you get my meaning."[24]

The Bantam paperback of the screenplay is labeled as "Robert Altman's Award-Winning *Nashville*" at the top of the front cover, and "With an Introduction by Joan Tewkesbury" at the bottom.[25] The only attribution of the screenplay to

Tewkesbury occurs in a small font on page 3. Otherwise, judging from the cover, Tewkesbury's contribution appears to be an introduction to a completed screenplay associated only with Robert Altman. Altman distributed the financial proceeds from the book to all twenty-four cast members due to their contributions to the script. This is a generous gesture, but, again, the screenwriter is marginalized at the expense of constructing Altman as the auteur. Altman's ability to turn actors' "improvisation to gold" overshadows the role of Joan Tewkesbury as the original creative force behind the film. The most favorable quote from Altman on the collaboration in *Nashville* still elides Tewkesbury: "*Nashville* is the best movie I've done because I've had the least to do with it. That's not meant to be generous. It's true."[26]

From Script to Screen

Tewkesbury's contribution to *Nashville*, separate from Altman's influence, can be appreciated through analyzing her screenplay and comparing the content and structure to the final film. Many drafts of the script exist and some of the major changes in the drafts have already been discussed. For this analysis, I am selecting a script (marked "Fourth Draft" and dated January 5, 1974) from far along in the development process. There are certainly many differences from the film, yet the structure and flow of action are close to those of Altman's film. Most striking, though, is the presence of a different voice in the screenplay, reflecting a much darker tone and engagement with social issues. In this way, the screenplay allows us to see Tewkesbury's vision and how this perspective is markedly different from Altman's looser and lighter approach to the material.

Deviating from typical screenplays, Tewkesbury's script has a great deal of background information on the characters, their pasts, and their motivations. Typically, this kind of detail is missing from a screenplay that is largely dependent on action and dialogue. In addition to the actor/improvisation angle, another talking point for the publicity could have been exploring this unusual deep dive into character within the script. This level of detail would influence an actor's conceptualization of the character and even their performance choices. Few have commented on Tewkesbury's extensive character descriptions in the *Nashville* screenplay, either at the time of release or in the decades since.

Consider, for example, Norman (played by David Arkin), the driver working for Bill, Mary, and Tom. He has a limited presence in the film, mainly as a foil for the three singers and to act as a befuddled and somewhat incompetent character. He does not motivate any significant action. In his most significant scene, Norman is slighted by Opal, who addresses him as "driver," drawing a class distinction that is more appropriate to England than the USA.

The screenplay introduces Norman with this lengthy narrative:

> *A young man, NORMAN BERGMAN, careens out. His father owns the only two delicatessens in Nashville, and, after not going into the delicatessen business, he has tried a lot of*

different kinds of education, smoking a lot of dope (which now makes him sick—everything pretty much makes him sick), trying to be a folk singer, and now working for Drive-U Service picking up artists and driving them around town. He wears a uniform of black trousers, maroon jacket and white shirt with black tie. Somehow it doesn't suit him, but he wears it anyway. Most often Norman is confused, and, therefore, too late or too early to appointments.

This setup explains why Norman is always somewhat out of place in every scene. The physical manifestation of his dislocation from vomiting at unfortunate moments recurs throughout the screenplay. Norman comes across as a confused young adult who simply cannot fit into the celebrity culture of Nashville. Tewkesbury does not make the character overly sympathetic; in fact, in one exchange, Norman openly expresses his racial prejudice. In the film, Norman plays a much smaller role, mainly reacting to the trio. His backstory and his physical ailments are missing. Nevertheless, actor David Arkin no doubt benefited from Tewkesbury's comprehensive picture of Norman.

Other characters, including Triplette, Albuquerque, Mr. Green, Haven Hamilton, and L.A. Joan, are also given rich histories, family descriptions, and psychological motivations within Tewkesbury's screenplay. Knowing, for instance, that Triplette "makes one think of white dinner jackets, Balboa California, Sigma Chi summer dances with paper lanterns and his mother's apple pie" gives a concise visual, cultural, and social summary of the character. These descriptions help

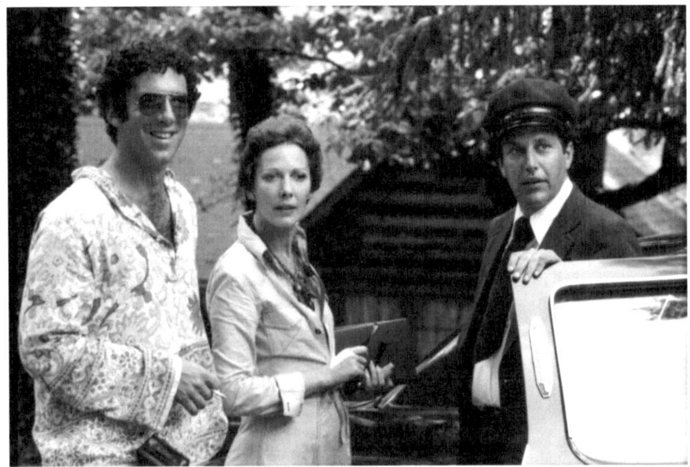

Figure 6: Norman (right), played by David Arkin, accompanied by Elliott Gould and publicist Sue Barton at Haven Hamilton's home.

considerably in situating each character within the *Nashville* landscape, and they supply enough detail to show the motivations for the characters' actions within the film.

The film was criticized by some in Nashville for offering a negative image of the country stars and their music. Tewkesbury's screenplay, however, is anchored much more clearly in the country music of that time. The screenplay begins in New York City where Tom Frank is picking up a gold record from his label, Columbia Records. Tom flirts with the secretary who hands him the gold record. He makes a quick comment about disliking flying, and the scene transitions to Haven Hamilton in Nashville recording a song. By opening with the New York City scene, Tewkesbury shows that country music was at a point of transition, becoming more commercial and with crossover artists becoming more prominent. Tom Frank, Bill and Mary are hardly country musicians.[27] They would be classified as folk, rock, or pop before aligning with country. The trio mirrors other musical artists of that time, such as John Denver and Olivia Newton-John, who were expanding the country audience through crossover music between genres. Tewkesbury pinpoints this inflection point in both country music and in the city of Nashville.

Tewkesbury also alludes to darker elements within the city, given its growth. In the screenplay, Opal talks with Triplette about the unsolved 1973 murder of legendary musician David 'Stringbean' Akeman, killed by two cousins looking for money (Stringbean kept all his money at home). The brutal violence creates shockwaves in the Nashville music scene. As Steven Paul described the impact, "The death of Stringbean Akeman ushered in a colossal, almost industry-wide shift in the country music world. The violent killings changed how the people making country music in Nashville lived. Some stars moved, others built fences and installed security, and all became more isolated and closed off."[28] The exchange about Stringbean in the screenplay is not included in Altman's film.

Citing the Stringbean murder reflects a tendency toward more serious content in the screenplay compared to the film. Although the dramatic situations are similar in both, Tewkesbury's screenplay has a bleaker worldview. She accurately describes this impulse in her comments during an AFI seminar: "So I will usually go for the murky; I would like to not be that way, as I tend to go into all the dark corners or turn over rocks to find out what those underthings are."[29]

Tewkesbury's approach is manifested through the character relationships and with deeper engagement with the social issues facing the country. In terms of the relationships, tensions evident in the film are emphasized to a much greater degree in the screenplay. Bill and Mary are shown to have a very toxic relationship that entails spousal abuse. In a ferocious scene, the couple slap each other violently and Mary retreats to the bathroom as Bill tries to force his way in. The next day, Mary's face is swollen from the attack. This dim view of relationships is also reflected in the screenplay with Barnett and Barbara Jean. We learn that Barnett actively avoids the advice of medical professionals in making Barbara Jean leave the hospital for a singing gig. The film implies that Barnett has sacrificed Barbara Jean's health to foster her career, but the screenplay makes this tie much more explicit. Consequently, Barbara Jean emerges as a more tragic figure, undermined directly by her husband/manager.

Tewkesbury's screenplay explores drug culture, racism, and sexual freedom, particularly within the context of the conservative southern city. Altman's film has a limited number of references to drugs. The most conspicuous scene involves Tom asking Norman to score some drugs for him. In Tewkesbury's screenplay, however, there is a thread of references to a wide range of recreational drugs. For some characters, this is accepted usage. When they first meet, Wade asks Linnea if she has ever done angel dust, a far cry from marijuana. In another difference from the film, the fight at Lady Pearl's bar is initi-

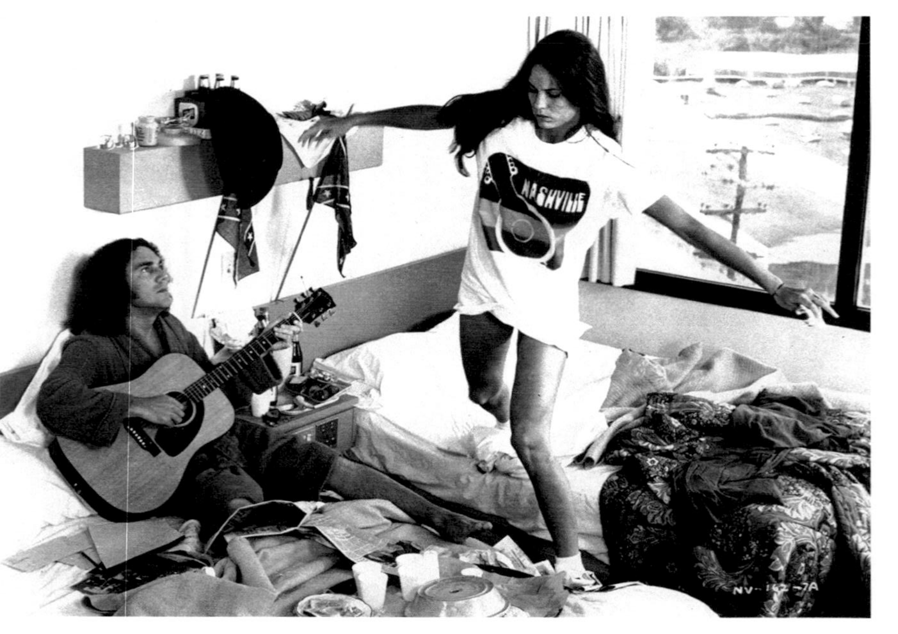

Figure 7: Bill and Mary’s fight in the hotel room had a more physical dimension in an earlier script draft.

ated by a joint being placed in a hat for tips. On discovering the joint, an outraged Lady Pearl exclaims, "I don't want no hippies in here!" As with drug culture, sharp references to racial bias appear throughout the screenplay. In the film, Wade, one of only two black characters, brings up issues related to race while the other characters do not address the topic.[30] Already an unlikable character for playing so many women against each other, in the screenplay, Tom Frank queries Linnea about sitting beside Wade at the Exit/In club: "Come on, you ever balled a black guy?" The remark underlines Tewkesbury's notion that race is a defining feature in the South and creates an even more negative image for the lothario Tom.

Altman portrays L.A. Joan as a trendy groupie, obsessed with seducing celebrities. She has few lines and is defined by her physical appearance and her dramatic changes in looks throughout the film. As Altman commented on Shelley Duvall's appearance as L.A. Joan, "In *Nashville*, she was a cartoon. That's what she was supposed to be."[31] In the Tewkesbury screenplay, L.A. Joan is more defined: she aspires to musical stardom, and in the most substantial difference, she is dealing with an unexpected pregnancy. Keeping in mind that *Nashville* was released just two years after the *Roe v. Wade* decision, Tewkesbury's scene of L.A. Joan getting an abortion gives the character much higher dramatic stakes than in the film. L.A. Joan gets Tom Frank to pay for her procedure: he drops her at the clinic and gives the nurse at the front desk $250 in bills. The film portrays consensual sexual dalliances as an accepted part of the contemporary scene. With L.A. Joan's abortion, Tewkesbury makes the viewer aware of the consequences of this sexual freedom. The scene is not moralizing, but it is a reminder of the wider social effects of sexual liberation, especially for women.

Other differences between screenplay and film are evident in findings from the film's contact sheets. The contact sheets in the archive reveal several scenes that would give the film greater continuity and the characters more depth. Tewkesbury's screenplay is constructed so that actions are motivated and there is a clear development of the dramatic stakes of each storyline. As with the contact sheets, the screenplay does connect the dots between events, leaving less room for viewers to construct their own visions of offscreen action. Although she does not sketch the reasons for Kenny's assassination, Tewkesbury does give the character more of a voice, even allowing him to speak after the shooting (he notes that his real target was Hal Phillip Walker). Walker is portrayed as a callous opportunist in the screenplay. After making a quip about Barbara Jean, who has just been killed, Triplette knocks Walker out. The exchange gives a satisfying emotional resolution and redeems the slippery Triplette.

If the screenplay is Tewkesbury's, the final film must be seen as shared between Altman, Tewkesbury, the actors, and the many creative collaborators working on *Nashville*. The film has greater levity, adding moments of satire, visual and verbal gags, and funny observations about daily life. The changes consistently favor a far less serious engagement with issues compared to Tewkesbury's screenplay. The writer notes that characters were softened by Altman, citing the Tricycle Man (Jeff Goldblum) as an example. Tewkesbury's original character had a more menacing appearance at odds with the conservative culture of Nashville:

> He was a much darker character based on someone that we had worked with in Mississippi during *Thieves Like Us*. He was a Hell's Angel and looked like a bug with these wide yellow sunglasses. The guy had a very souped up tricycle, long hair and some people just did not like him. Bob saw Jeff Goldblum and his comedy routine, and Bob fell in love with him, and suddenly the tricycle man became an object of literal magic, which was too bad because the character lost its edge.[32]

The Tricycle Man, by his strong presence, alleviated bad situations, such as Del Reese aggressively flirting with Sueleen after her appearance at the fundraiser. Reese, scared by the Tricycle Man, scurries away and leaves Sueleen to return to her home. In the film, the Tricycle Man is an innocuous force, extravagantly dressed and limited to doing brief magic tricks to entertain other characters.

The humor in the film takes many forms. Principally, and largely missing from the script, Altman privileges brief moments of off-center humor, sometimes highlighting a character's dislocation: Mr. Green excusing his niece ("She's from California"); Opal's many bizarre analogies for explaining the USA (the yellow buses, the graveyard of cars, the freeway accident); Triplette's jabs at Haven's height and Connie White's dress; Haven making the random leap from the New Christy Minstrels to Julie Christie; Linnea's hyperbolic description of motorcycle accidents. Rather than comic gags, these examples are character-centered and are funny for their observations. They speak to humor occurring in everyday life, not in a scripted comedy. Critics much less often mention the physical or sight gags in *Nashville*: the parking lot barrier being destroyed, the freeway accident caused by a canoe falling on the road, two cars colliding as Albuquerque blithely walks by, the speedway drowning out Maysie and Albuquerque singing, Bud failing to recognize L.A. Joan after she changes wigs, and the plastic guns twirled by the majorettes to welcome Barbara Jean at the airport.

Some music might also generate laughter, especially the songs from Haven Hamilton (Henry Gibson). The first number, "200 Years," could be taken at face value, as a patriotic endorsement of the USA. The song might easily be interpreted as a satirical indictment of the historical markers of the country. Gibson's overly earnest performance and the lyrics add to this reading. Even the refrain, "We must be doing something right to last 200 years," is qualified and tentative: the big accomplishment for the country is "doing something right"? Haven's Opry song "For the Sake of the Children" feels more broadly satirical with its sanctimonious lyrics of a philanderer telling his mistress that he must return to his children ("Jimmy, Kathy and Sweet Lorelei"). Corny, simplistic, and plodding, the song would elicit laughter more often than an emotional connection. Part of *Nashville*'s challenge is to integrate this cringe-inducing song with the more heartfelt, rousing country songs of Ronee Blakley (e.g., "My Idaho Home," "Dues," "Tapedeck in His Tractor").

The lighter elements in *Nashville* point to Altman more

than Tewkesbury. These aspects make the film more audience-friendly, bolstering the entertainment quotient and helping the viewer through the dense fabric of the film's composition. In this way, Altman's sensibility did have a populist bent. Tewkesbury commented about Altman's work in *Nashville*, "He wanted to be a popular filmmaker. He wouldn't go the distance in some areas."[33] Altman proclaimed that *Nashville* was a popular film, although in interviews later during the film's distribution, he acknowledged that the film failed to live up to box office expectations.[34] Nevertheless, it is unusual to think about Altman courting audience interest, because so much of his work is idiosyncratic and offbeat. Tewkesbury's claim about Altman's desire to be popular can be seen in later projects as well. His bleak postapocalyptic drama *Quintet* (1979), set in a barren arctic landscape and based around an undecipherable death game, feels more like a bleak Ingmar Bergman drama, yet the director attempted to build interest in the film through developing a board game for Kenner Toys.[35] Eventually Kenner and Twentieth Century-Fox decided not to move forward with the game, thinking that it would not help marketing the film and could even hurt promotion in Europe (where Altman was held in high regard as a film artist).

Joan and Bob

Although the collaboration between the two blurs the contributions of each, Tewkesbury must be credited for the structure, depth of character, and engagement with social issues in *Nashville*. Altman shifted the screenplay through the assassi-

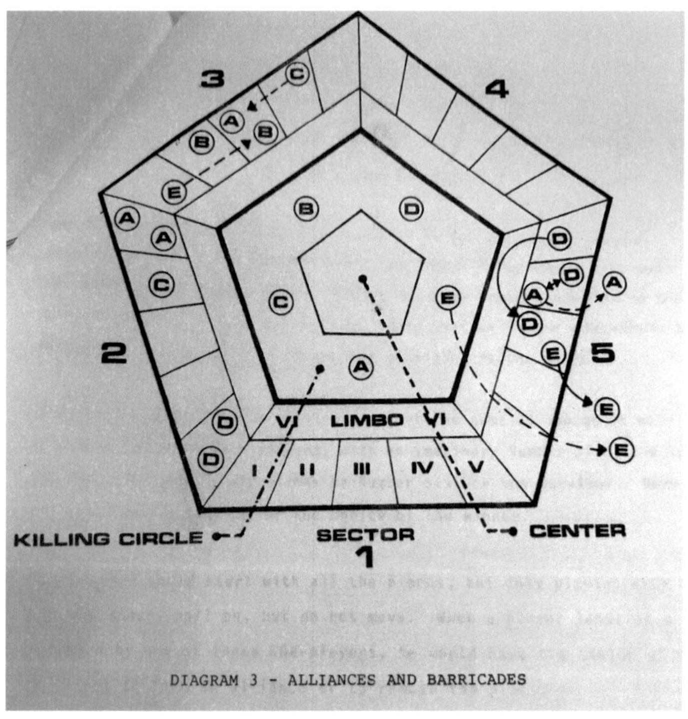

Figure 8: *Quintet* board game outline.

nation ending and the addition of the political thread. Additionally, much of the jaundiced perspective on life, the satire, and the humor connect directly to Altman. Finding the specific moment to encapsulate a character or situation is an Altman talent evident in *Nashville* and many of his other films. Alan Rudolph confirms that Altman would privilege an unexpected addition in a scene if it made a point and moved the film forward. As a result, *Nashville* grew and expanded on Tewkesbury's screenplay when, to use Rudolph's example, "a throw-away line delivered more contribution than an entire scene."[36] Summing up the collaboration on *Nashville*, Tewkesbury pinpoints their individual strengths: "My tendency is to go down very far. Altman likes to stay up there on the surface."[37]

Tewkesbury and Altman brought complementary skills to the film: Tewkesbury invested in character and Altman masterfully sketched a landscape of people, sounds, settings, and events small and large. For Tewkesbury, character is action while Altman delights in everyday moments revealing the human condition. Both strengths result in *Nashville*'s continuing relevancy and value as a film and social text. Several other Altman social-landscape films, such as *A Wedding* and *Health* (1980), failed to cohere because the structure and characterization could not match those in Tewkesbury's *Nashville* screenplay. Her work in the film has been undervalued in deference to Altman's auteur image. I hope that this chapter illuminates how the in-depth screenplay and Tewkesbury's collaboration with Altman throughout the production process helped to shape the film.

Tewkesbury's visibility as screenwriter was not impacted only by Altman building his image. An even more pervasive influence was the sexism of the film industry during that era. Tewkesbury wanted to parlay her collaboration with Altman into a directing career. Altman was open to the idea of serving as producer for a film directed by her. Unfortunately, the team could not garner any commitments from the studios. At the same time, Altman was able to sponsor Alan Rudolph's initial venture as a director, *Welcome to L.A.* (1976).

Decades later, Tewkesbury sees this contrast as indicative of the deep sexism within the industry. As she commented on this industry dynamic, "In the power structure, your role was the girl."[38] Without Altman's endorsement, Tewkesbury nevertheless forged a career as a director, beginning with *Old Boyfriends* (1979), and she continued her work as a writer and director over the next three decades. Although she worked on a screenplay for Altman's aborted film version of *Ragtime* and remained friends with Altman, the pair did not collaborate again on a film project.

CHAPTER 3

Nashville's Americana

Nashville is a mirror of the United States of America, not simply a reflection of the country-music capital. This conceit is expressed in many ways: the American flag contained in the film's poster title; the film's red, white, and blue color scheme; the social cross-section of the film's characters; and in a recording session right at the beginning, Haven Hamilton extolling the virtues of America's "200 Years." Reviewers in 1975 certainly picked up on this connection, proclaiming that Altman was making a statement about America in addition to (or instead of) any analysis of country music and the town of Nashville. *Nashville* is a bicentennial work, and his next film, *Buffalo Bill and the Indians, or Sitting Bull's History Lesson*, continued his investigation into the corrosive effect of American institutions and the American dream.[1]

Many critics have referenced *Nashville* as a metaphor for America, but few, with the important exception of Helene Keyssar, have described the parameters of Altman's America.[2] *Nashville* has been acclaimed as a high point in the New Hollywood era; its longevity is linked not just to its aesthetic achievements but to the prescience of its politics and the penetrating social landscape captured by the film. This analysis of the film's Americana is built through reference to artifacts from the Altman archive. These threads evidence the importance of commerce, image management, and exploitation in America. If the American dream existed when *Nashville* was made, Altman clearly believed that these were factors bolstering any kind of achievement in America.

Political: Hal Phillip Walker and New Roots for America

Joan Tewkesbury drafted her initial screenplay for *Nashville* without the political throughline. Altman added this element, which grew as a significant thread tying the film together. Altman commissioned author Thomas Hal Phillips to construct a political campaign as a background for the film.[3] Altman's only caveat was that Phillip's candidate must be someone whom Phillips would want to vote for and who could actually be elected.[4] Phillips's background evidenced both social liberalism (he authored a gay romantic novel *Bitterweed Path* in 1950) and conservatism (he ran the Republican campaign for his younger brother Rubel Phillips). In his role as the first chairman of the Mississippi Film Commission, Thomas Hal Phillips encountered Altman during the shooting of *Thieves Like Us*. The connection between Phillips and the director continued after *Nashville*, with Phillips playing Hal Phillip Walker in Altman's *O.C. & Stiggs* in 1983.

Hal Phillip Walker's Replacement Party campaign pitch runs throughout *Nashville*, primarily through the loudspeakers on Walker's van, almost always in the background of exterior shots. A bevy of young female Walker campaigners, dressed in red, white, and blue, are also present, waving Walker bumper stickers and cajoling residents to vote for Walker. The campaign is branded with the phrase "New Roots for the Nation," accompanied by the graphic of the USA covered by a tree and its (new) roots. As J. Hoberman points out, "new roots for the nation" is an oxymoron—a satirical take no doubt intended by Phillips and Altman.

Altman's archive contains three primary materials on Hal Phillip Walker: a campaign brochure summarizing key talking points for the candidate, a document titled "The Man" offering an extensive personal biography of Walker, and another document, "The Candidate," lacing together the personal experience with the policy statements and perspectives. Although much of this material is not made explicit in the film, clearly Phillips used this background to shape the candidate's campaign and his reactionary stance to most contemporary politics.

The biography of Hal Phillip Walker, born in 1922 in North Carolina, is marked by the importance of family, the value of patriotism, and most of all, the rewards for ingenuity and entrepreneurship. He spent his youth working on the family farm inherited from his grandfather. Walker interrupts his college studies in farm management to serve in World War II. As a part of the amphibious forces, Walker becomes a Purple Heart recipient and later serves in the Pentagon as a personnel officer. After completing his degree, Walker moves from managing the farm to stepping in for his ailing father to lead his electrical contracting business. Within a few years, Walker builds the local company into the leading global provider of

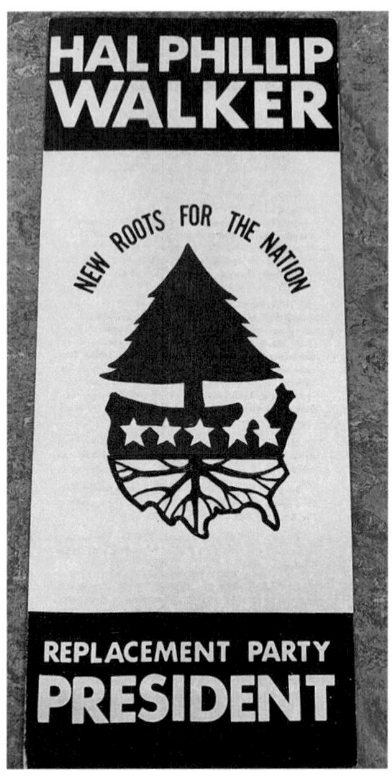

Figure 9: Hal Phillip Walker pamphlet.

high-power electrical transmission lines. With financial security in place, Walker starts to give back to society with large-scale efforts for the United Fund Drive. He dips his finger into politics first by serving as a special representative to the Kennedy Round Tariff Talks in Geneva. As part of this initiative, Walker facilitates international trade of farm products and machinery to developing countries. The political commitment deepens as Walker became the Democratic governor of North

Carolina, receiving the largest popular vote ever bestowed on a North Carolina state official. Neither of the Walker background documents explains why the candidate abandoned the Democratic party to form his own third-party organization, the Replacement Party. Walker gives a legendary graduation address to Duke University in 1971. The central talking points of the speech, which became known as the "New Roots" speech, became the tenets of Walker's Replacement Party.

The leading statement in Walker's candidate profile signals one potential reason for his disenchantment from the Democrats: "Hal Phillip Walker understands the unique problems facing the farmers today. Having been raised on a farm and schooled in farm management he brings to the American farmer not only a firsthand knowledge of their problems but a positive pay-for-doing program to replace the failures of pay-for-not-doing subsidies." Privileging hard work and ingenuity over government support is a recurring theme in the Walker literature. While Ken Dancyger states that Hal Phillip Walker wants to abolish the role of government in American life, Walker's message is more about lowering the governmental presence and increasing oversight of governmental officials.[5] Walker wants government to play a smaller role in everyday life. He prides himself on finding redundancies in current programs: "As Governor he combined government agencies and instituted a central purchasing department reducing the net cost of government by 8%." Further, Walker was so successful in applying his business acumen to his governorship that he transformed a $28 million dollar deficit into a $51 million dollar surplus.

The Replacement Party is obsessed with one specific kind of replacement: as Walker describes it, his mission is "to replace lawyeristic-legalistic government with the common sense of farmers, teachers, engineers, and businessmen and women." As often heard from the Walker vans careening through the city, lawyers obscure the truth and confuse listeners. As Walker recounts, "Have you ever asked a lawyer for the time? He told you how to make a watch." Walker also points out how lawyers make up more than half of Congress, even though, as Walker argues, they are woefully unequipped to set policy or to represent the lives and concerns of common people. For Walker, anything touched by lawyers is immediately suspect. He even wants to replace the national anthem, which "nobody knows the words or can sing," because it was written by a lawyer and voted into acceptance by lawyers.

Fostering a strong populist message, Walker wants lawyers to be replaced by everyday people, especially those who have proven their worth by hard work and diligence. The populism of Walker's message has been interpreted as a panacea for the masses: Steven Abrahams sees this as "an appeal to the common man's sense of frustration," while J. Hoberman characterizes Walker as leveling-down politics, "the cheerful negation of complicated realities."[6]

How politicians will be replaced with the voice of the everyday person is much less clear in the Walker rhetoric. There are complications and contradictions inherent in the Walker campaign. For instance, despite claiming that the government should play a smaller role overall, Walker advocates strongly for increased internal monitoring within the USA:

"Security should be the first and last design of all government: Security of mind, of health, of heart. I can think of no sensible reason why New York must have 12,000 major crimes for every 1,000 crimes committed in Tokyo." The limits of freedom for Walker are reflected in the need to police and control individuals. Walker's call to action sounds a lot like George W. Bush's Department of Homeland Security, instituted after the 9/11 terrorist attacks.

Interestingly, Walker does not align with any religious interests. In fact, he wants to tax churches on their land and corporate investments. There is still a liberal thread to Walker's agenda: he argues for government to intervene with national healthcare, shows concern for regulating pollution, and defends the freedom of the press and their role in exposing abuses of trust in government. In a policy statement that resonates many decades later, Walker denounces the electoral college as "a flagrant violation" of the one-man one-vote rule.

Religion and politics are nevertheless laced together in Altman's film. The most explicit political analysis (or monologue) is by Lady Pearl, club owner and lover of Haven Hamilton. At her club, Altman starts the scene on a huge photographic poster of John Kennedy and then pans across the expanse of her country-and-western saloon. This shot anticipates Pearl's lengthy explanation of her connection to "the Kennedy boys" while talking with Opal at the King of the Road nightclub. Does Pearl express her admiration for a political agenda or platform by the Kennedys? Not at all. In fact, the speech appears to claim that anti-Catholicism is at the root of John Kennedy's loss in Tennessee. Taking a sharp swipe at Baptists, Lady Pearl bases her love for the Kennedys on their religious affiliation.[7]

Walker's campaign is taking place in an America shell-shocked by a whole battery of issues: Watergate, distrust of American institutions, stagflation, gas shortages, the struggles for civil rights among the disenfranchised. With the lack of faith in government to represent everyday people, *Nashville* shows how those still struggling to achieve economic and social stability have been denied a voice. Walker's folksy appeal and commitment to the common man over experts, professionals, and government officials clearly tap into a chord in the country at that time.

Nashville actor Keith Carradine considers Altman's foresight in anticipating the political landscape to be a considerable achievement. As Carradine explains, "The great artists see who we are becoming more so than seeing who we are."[8] Elements of the Walker campaign and the unmet needs of the American voter resonate for much of the next five decades. Indeed, Jimmy Carter's campaign in 1976 reflects many of the Walker's concerns. Aaron Latham draws the deepest parallels between the two: from both being southern farmers and successful businessmen to proclaiming the strong belief that Americans are resilient in the face of challenges and disappointments.[9] Carter had a savvy connection with the media, being able to tap into American popular culture through sound-bites that play on basic emotions and values.[10] Hal Phillip Walker also resonates through several other candidates over the subsequent decades: Ronald Reagan's feel-good optimism and foundational belief in America circa 1980, Ross

Perot's third-party candidacy in 1992, Bill Clinton's southern charm, and Donald Trump's ability to tap into the dissatisfaction of the everyman while being disruptive to traditional political norms and ideological beliefs.

It is important to remember that the political messaging in *Nashville* is presented intermittently and in short bursts, with many interruptions as the Walker van travels through the city. Director Wim Wenders makes the astute comment that *Nashville* is "a film about noise, that particularly American noise of music and talking and traffic and commercials on radio and television."[11] David Sterritt perfectly captures how Walker's campaign operates through sentiments that ultimately leave the listener puzzled: "Although we never lay eyes on Walker, we hear a good deal of his spiel from his peripatetic sound track, as, for instance, 'When you pay more for an automobile than it cost for Columbus to make his first voyage to America, that's politics.' To which one might respond, when you pretend such a nonsensical statement means something, *that's* politics."[12]

Walker's campaign is simply one more element of noise in the film. Characters are continually exposed to Walker's message, but very few talk about the candidate or his platform. Instead, characters express a fondness for past political candidates (Lady Pearl's love for John and Robert Kennedy), a neutrality (Haven Hamilton sponsoring all political candidates), or an ambivalence that can be leveraged to Walker (Bill's commitment to the Walker rally as a chance to bolster his trio's media image). As Peter Lev sums up the situation, "in the film we see no interest in political ideas or positions."[13]

We never glimpse Hal Phillip Walker; we only hear his voice and see his campaign stickers and promotional items. This absence is telling. Rather than focus on Walker, the audience is exposed to Walker's operative, the smooth-talking Triplette (Michael Murphy). While *Nashville* is often characterized as episodic and narratively diffuse, Mark Minett argues that Triplette's mission to gather talent for the political rally is the driver of the narrative. Triplette does have a goal—to secure talent for the Walker rally in Nashville—and his storyline follows this mission. The rally opens with the biggest stars, Barbara Jean and Haven Hamilton, with an array of others waiting to perform, including Tommy Brown; Bill, Mary, and Tom; and Linnea with the Fisk University choir. Triplette functions as a shapeshifter: morphing his pitch and style of delivery to the target he is interested in landing for the rally. For Haven, he offers Walker's support if Hamilton wants to run for governor of Tennessee. For Barbara Jean, his commitment is limited, as Barbara Jean's truncated Opry Belle performance leaves manager/husband Barnett wanting to schedule another gig as a replacement. Triplette must only agree to let her sing first and exit before Walker takes the stage. For Bill and Mary, Triplette promises extended exposure, as the rally will be a syndicated television special. Triplette also tells Bill that the trio will stand out against the "local yokels" of country music on the bill.

Another replacement takes place. Altman's role for Triplette rather than Hal Phillip Walker as the center is particularly noteworthy.[14] Altman implies that Triplette, the man behind the candidate, is more significant than the politician.

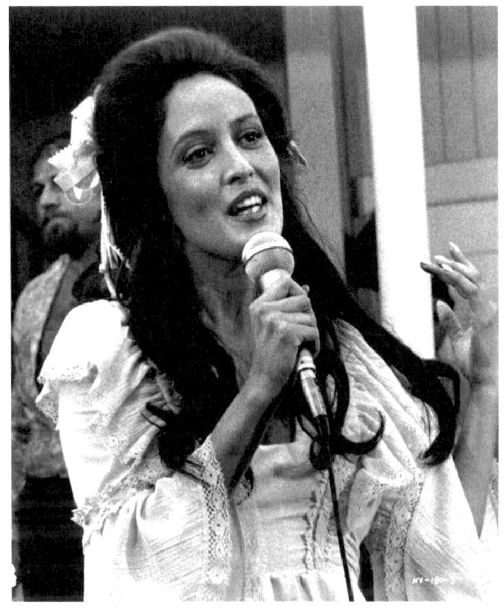

Figure 10: Barbara Jean's truncated appearance at the Opry Belle leads to Barnett promising that she will appear at the political rally.

Politics becomes a function of image, commerce, and marketing. Triplette is not invested in politics. He is just a facilitator, or as Peter Lev describes him, "purely a deal maker."[15] Notice how Triplette never presents Walker's positions on issues; he is only interested in explaining how appearing at the rally can have a positive impact on each of the performers (or targets, to use a marketing term). So, aligning with Walker is repositioned as bolstering a star image and album sales, and enabling others to enter the arena of power politics. In the replacement (party), politics has been exchanged for commerce.

The politics/commerce connection is bridged through entertainment, in this case, country music. Altman explicitly makes the equation between politics and country music as central to the design of the film: "our political, our elected officials . . . are also hard to shake once they get up there. And their speeches are no different than the country-western songs—each new song doesn't really say anything. And that's pretty much how this thing started—the idea of making that comparison."[16] The quote does not mean that Altman sees the political platforms and country music as empty or devoid of value. Rather, both contain pithy, easily digested, and simple platitudes that empower and guide the listener/voter. These sentiments situate each person in our society while endorsing a set of values that, while seemingly neutral, yields control to those in political power.

The intersection of politics, commerce, and entertainment forges a new presidential figure, tagged by Kathryn Cramer Brownell as the entertainer in chief or the performative president. Brownell traces the celebrity president from John Kennedy through Barack Obama; these are political figures who can use the tools of entertainment to transform public perceptions of their presidency.[17] The period around *Nashville*'s release evidenced the growing importance of the performative president. Richard Nixon said "Sock it to me!" on *Laugh-In* to court younger voters (despite his disapproval of the hip, satirical show).[18] Nixon's replacement, Gerald Ford, struggled to counter Chevy Chase's depiction of him on *Saturday Night Live* as bumbling and ineffectual. Ron Nessen, Ford's White House press secretary, even hosted *Saturday Night Live* hoping to lighten the image of Ford and to show Ford's sense of humor. Brownell views this moment as evidence of "the rise of the entertainer in chief and the constant demands for image construction and performative skills that this presidential function demanded."[19]

Altman brings together politics, commerce, and show business, showing how all three have an impact on our daily lives. Could *Nashville* be characterized solely as a political film? I think this claim is more difficult to make. As Christos Tsiolkas suggests about the labeling, "Was the multicharacter political allegory of *Nashville* so radical compared to Jean-Luc Godard or Straub-Huillet?"[20] In Godard's *2 or 3 Things I Know About Her* (1967), for instance, within the first few minutes the director, through his own voice-over, introduces a barrage of images, ideas, and sounds connected to exploitation, commerce, and gender. From the data on the expansion of Paris for financial reasons to actress Marina Vlady's status as an object for erotic enjoyment, *2 or 3 Things* spills over with political and social ideas. The narrative is episodic in the extreme, secondary to the political thoughts that Godard continuously disperses.

With Altman, the political campaign of Hal Phillip Walker is mostly represented by Walker's voice blaring from his vans crisscrossing the city. While this aural element could be seen as Brechtian, breaking the world of the film for political commentary, it becomes instead just more noise, to invoke Wenders's term. Altman's approach to politics is closer to observation than direct critique. With the documentary feel of the shooting, the natural dialogue, and the presence of multiple characters in a single setting, a finer political message can be found on dissecting the characters and interactions. The political background is crucial for adding context and framing to the film. The sharply drawn lives and portrayals of the characters uncover Altman's viewpoint on American society and how, as Pauline Kael comments, all of us are complicit in the lie of America.

Social: Gender and Race in *Nashville*

The array of characters paints a picture of Altman's take on gender and race in American society at that time. As with so much of the film, complications are evident in these depictions. At most, we can identify some ideological threads that illustrate how gender and race function in Altman's America.

Although Altman, with Joe/Joanne in *Come Back to the Five and Dime, Jimmy Dean, Jimmy Dean* (1983), offered one of the first positive trans representations in film, in *Nashville*, gender is constructed firmly in binary terms.[21] The male characters in *Nashville* are defined through their professions or jobs (Barnett, manager; Triplette, political aide; Norman, chauffeur; Wade, cook; Del, lawyer; Bud, business manager; Mr. Green, retired; Pvt. Kelly, military) and/or their connection to music industry (Bill, Tom, Haven, Tommy Brown).[22] Each male character is predominantly labeled with their job function, which places them in the social hierarchy of *Nashville*, with Haven Hamilton as the most significant figure and the transient characters of Star and the Tricycle Man falling at the bottom of the list.

Helene Keyssar makes the pointed observation that "Nashville the city is controlled by men but the film is made whole and compelling by its women."[23] This sentiment was not shared widely, though. David Sterritt, following several other critics, sees the film offering points of ridicule and humiliation of certain female characters, or, as Sterritt terms it, "Altman's own susceptibility to gender bias."[24] Looking at the female characters in a larger social context highlights how the intersection of politics, commerce, and show business shapes the conditions and experiences of each person. Rather than highlight how second-wave feminism was shifting roles and power for women in that decade, the film foregrounds how gender was stuck in an earlier era in a southern city such as Nashville.

Tellingly, while the male characters are mostly set in their social place, many of *Nashville*'s women are presented as chasing the American dream, often with stardom and fame as the end goal. Unlike most of the male characters, the women are more likely to be disenfranchised, searching for position and value. Many of these women see fame as currency, believing that becoming a music celebrity will achieve all their dreams. Sueleen and Albuquerque are the most obvious examples; they are unlikely singers without adequate support to showcase their talents. Altman often places both characters in the same location (e.g., the traffic accident, the Demon's Den nightclub, the political fundraiser), making the viewer connect them and their shared mission of achieving stardom. The ending illustrates the arbitrary nature of becoming a star: Albuquerque is handed the microphone randomly by Haven, and, being in the right place at the right time, she uses the opportunity to sing boldly, rousing the crowd and bringing peace back to the tragic scene. Sueleen, with little singing talent, is exploited by

Triplette and Del, who coerce her into stripping at the fundraiser. Albuquerque, with ample talent, only gets a chance to display her abilities through a rare set of circumstances. Otherwise, she too would be relegated to singing at the speedway, competing for attention with the noisy hotrods. Apart from Sueleen and Albuquerque, Connie White, who is already famous, seeks to bolster her celebrity and fandom, moving into the same realm as Barbara Jean.

Another set of female characters is fame-adjacent, in positions next to the famous rather than seeking recognition for themselves. L.A. Joan, formerly Martha, avoids visiting her sick aunt by pursuing an array of well-known men, from Bud Hamilton to Tom and, in the film's finale, Bill. Opal, supposedly working on a documentary about Nashville for the BBC, values celebrity above all else. In a particularly nasty moment, she sprints from Bud Hamilton, who is singing a gentle love song, just so she can sidle up to Elliott Gould. Both Opal and L.A. Joan show the dark side of trying to achieve the American dream: L.A. Joan uses her sexuality to gain favor, and Opal moves toward the stars in a predatory manner, ignoring all the signs that she is unwanted or misunderstood.

Nashville's portrayal of gender cannot, however, be simply characterized by these fame-seeking women struggling to move forward.[25] In fact, two characters, Linnea (Lily Tomlin) and Barbara Jean (Ronee Blakley), offer remarkably complex portrayals of people negotiating patriarchy, showing the multiple challenges of being female in America of the mid-1970s. Linnea is able to create a space for herself separate from her expected role as homemaker and mother. Altman presents

Linnea as a person of integrity and social conscience. She is a gospel singer, the only white member of a black choir. Linnea takes an active interest in facilitating the growth and development of her deaf children (recall that her husband has not bothered to learn sign language, so he cannot communicate with his own kids). Linnea can slip between these different roles effortlessly. Linnea's decision to sleep with Tom is the most intriguing aspect of her character. Linnea at first seems to rebuff Tom's advances, but after repeated calls, she meets him at the Exit/In club. Why does she acquiesce? Altman merely presents the scene without suggesting any cause and effect. From the earlier action, it seems possible that her marriage with Del is broken or even that they lead separate lives apart from their family obligations. We just know that Linnea is a self-assured character who declines to stay with Tom for the night after their assignation. She seeks pleasure on her own terms. Her actions fail to match the stereotype of the obedient southern suburban wife. Tomlin's performance enhances this more complicated characterization.

In reviews, Barbara Jean was often described as emotionally frail and unstable. Barnett's tirade in the hospital room suggests her character's past mental health challenges: "Are you goin' nutsy on me: Is that what you're doing? 'Cause I won't stand for that, Barbara Jean? You havin' one of them nervous breakdowns?" The understanding of mental health issues was rudimentary in 1975. Rather than posit a binary of well/unwell, it is more useful to consider the many factors at play in creating Barabra Jean's character. Altman, Tewkesbury, and Blakley make a character who is seriously exploited by her handlers and the music industry; she is commodified and minimized in the process. Barnett's strong language and shouting would now be considered abusive, but at the time of release, few mentioned that element.

The most productive way to consider Barbara Jean is to contrast her public and her private appearances. On stage, Barbara Jean sings, with confidence and conviction, of her past and her treasured family ("My Idaho Home"), of living a simple country life ("Tapedeck in His Tractor"), and, most poignantly, about her emotional disappointments and personal trauma ("It hurts so bad, it gets me down, down, down / I want to walk away from the battleground / This hurtin' life, it ain't no good"). Barbara Jean becomes so focused on each song that she goes into a reverie. In this trance she can live in the world of the song. Compare Barbara Jean's singing with her daily life, filled with commotion, endless demands, and strife with her husband and manager Barnett.

The shattering scene of Barbara Jean singing, then becoming lost in memories on the Opry Belle stage, combines her professional and personal worlds. She attempts to integrate past and present through recounting her childhood memories. Trying to draw the audience closer, she eventually gets lost in the past, forgetting to focus on the singing and placating her fans. The scene illustrates how the ongoing demands made by her manager/husband and the music industry take such a toll that Barbara Jean eventually cannot even function. Whether through fainting or dissolving into her dream world, Barbara Jean takes solace in her illness to cope with her exploitation. In economics, a public good, available to all, inevitably leads to overuse and neglect. *Nashville* offers the public good of Barbara Jean: a person whose needs, physical and emotional, are repressed or ignored. When Barbara Jean argues with Barnett in her hospital room, she is either trying to create space for her recovery or to distance herself from her husband. Sadly, she fails to reach both goals. Linnea has agency and control in her life, while Barbara Jean, the biggest star and moneymaker in *Nashville*, is manipulated and exploited and has little ability to guide her own destiny. These more nuanced perspectives on female characters, one progressive and one regressive, complicate the other trope of women striving for fame, fortune, and the American dream. Altman's women in *Nashville*, as Keyssar suggests, can create a vibrant and memorable locus for the film's action.

Gender divides roles and expectations in *Nashville*, but it is still possible for women to strive for control and power. Altman's view of race is more pessimistic. The two black characters, Wade, the short-order cook, and singer Tommy Brown, illustrate how America contained and marginalized black people, regardless of their class status. Wade is fascinating partly because he is the only character unafraid to tell difficult truths to those around him. Being brutally honest in a town (and country) of artifice makes Wade an outsider, accentuating the alienation he already feels as a person of color living in the South. Wade has only a few scenes, but notice how often he is able to break through convention and accepted fictions. When Sueleen wants to stay at the airport in case Barbara Jean will sing, Wade responds in a huff, "She don't sing unless she gets paid!" Speaking truth to power, a drunken Wade later confronts Tommy Brown, calling him "the whitest n***ger in town," a proclamation that causes a fight to break out in the club. In a very poignant scene, on learning that Sueleen was forced to do a striptease rather than sing, Wade tells her, "You may as well face the fact that you cannot sing." Sueleen simply dismisses Wade's heartfelt message quickly. For Wade, Nashville equals rejection and missed opportunities. As the crowd is gathering for Walker's rally, Wade can be seen driving away, soon to leave for his new home, Detroit. Jean Pagliuso's publicity shot of Robert Doqui as Wade offers a small redemption: smiling broadly in bright tan clothes and a sparkling golden necklace, Wade looks exuberant, happy, and confident.

Wade is either ignored or rejected, but black singer Tommy Brown figures prominently in the film as both an entertainer and an accepted part of the community. He is, however, continually reduced to one characteristic: his race. In the fourth script draft (dated January 1974), the only missing character is Tommy Brown. A character labeled as "black male singer" is included fleetingly, perhaps an inspiration for the final character, but there is also a hint that blackness is his defining quality. Many times throughout the film, Tommy Brown's appearance is linked directly to blackness: Opal fails to recognize Tommy in his own bus and blathers on about the place of black people in the South; Haven softly remarks, "You're lucky to be alive" as Tommy leaves the Opry stage; Haven offers watermelon to Tommy at the Speedway; and even Barbara Jean refers to Tommy as a "big black butterfly" when she greets him in the hospital.[26]

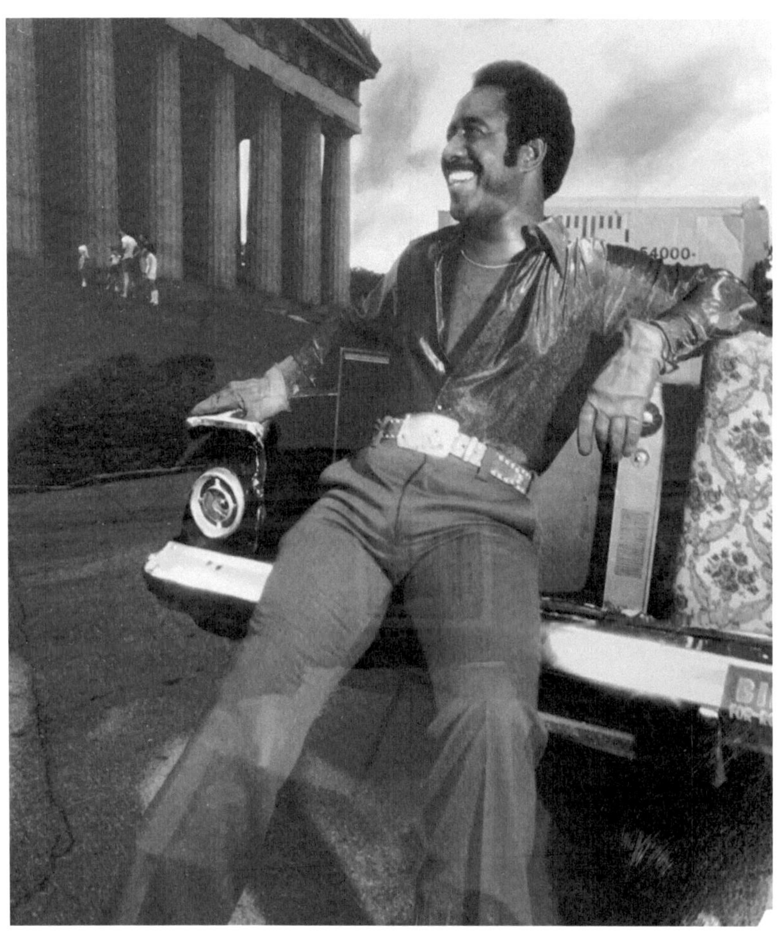

Figure 11: A glamor shot of Wade (Robert Doqui).

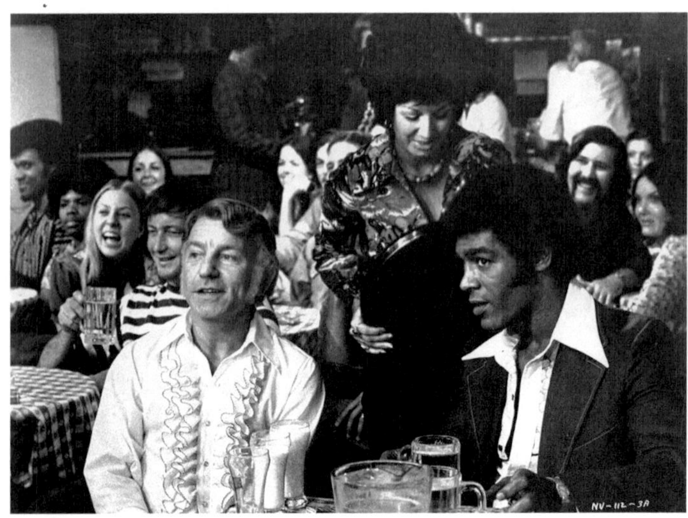

Figure 12: Tommy Brown (Timothy Brown) endures racist slurs at a club.

Altman includes scenes of Triplette trying to enlist Haven and Barbara Jean for the rally, but does not approach Tommy Brown. Tommy is standing on the Parthenon stage, so he is clearly scheduled to perform, yet Altman has not shown any interactions between Triplette and Tommy Brown (recall that Triplette has met with Haven, Barnett, Bill, and Mary to negotiate their appearances). Why is this negotiation scene missing for Tommy Brown? The oversight seems telling—it would be one moment in which Tommy would have some agency and be defined beyond his race. Other scenes giving the character a stronger presence were trimmed from the film, including Brown's second number at the Opry and an extended scene between Opal and Tommy.

As Jan Stuart comments on these trims, "(Timothy) Brown was painfully aware that a disproportionate amount of his work ended up on the cutting room floor."[27]

Altman offers a slightly more optimistic view of racial divisions in an element bracketing the film, the Fisk University gospel choir. The group is seen with Linnea in the film's opening as Bud escorts Opal to a recording studio next to his father's. The film moves from the white country music superstar to a black gospel choir with a white lead singer, Linnea. Robert Niemi illustrates the contrast between these two domains: "The hegemonic culture is moneyed, male-dominated, white, irascible and politically conservative while its subaltern cultures, mostly non-white and far less affluent, are demonstrably more egalitarian in their politics. Admittedly, Linnea Reese's role in the choir affirms white privilege but it also challenges patriarchy and she and the Fisk Jubilee Choir transgress Southern racist segregationist taboos by singing side-by-side in exuberant harmony."[28] The same choir joins Albuquerque singing on the Parthenon stage, responding to the opening by accompanying another white female singer. Richard Ness views this finale as transformative, opening the way for previously marginalized elements to gain control and offer an alternative to patriarchal order.[29] Possibly, although I think that in both the opening and the closing, presenting a black choir following the lead of a white singer can also be seen as just another means of group control and manipulation, albeit with the usual gender roles reversed.

America is a land of inequities, divided by gender, race, social class, and many other factors. Altman's film mirrors this perfectly with a stable set of male figures defined by their professions, women who are striving to better their lot in life, and people of color who are marginalized across the spectrum of social classes. Success is achieved through deal making and negotiation. Talent is valuable only insofar as it can be commoditized and sold, with stardom resulting largely from arbitrary circumstances. If, as Haven Hamilton sings, we must be doing something right to last 200 years, this achievement is at the expense of different groups who can be leveraged to support the status quo and the engine of American capitalism.

Commerce: The Film and Its Lessons

Altman's America is evident not only textually through the film and its elements, but also in the life of the film from Altman's archives. These archival documents reveal useful economic lessons that are also reflected in the film, attesting to the importance of artistic reinvention and image management. Unsurprisingly, Altman's archive contains, among many other items, material related to potential lawsuits and legal contracts connected to the film. An archive, of course, would be the most appropriate place to deposit anything connected to the legal or economic lives of the film. These items highlight aspects of the film's production, distribution, and marketing while filling in more details on Altman's perspective on America.

The ability for culture to be recycled, repurposed, and represented connects to the first set of documents concerning a potential lawsuit against Henry Gibson. Prior to *Nash-*

ville, Gibson was most famous for appearing in the groundbreaking *Laugh-In*. Essaying several roles on the show, Gibson, holding a giant daisy with a blank affect, was best known for reciting verse—satirical, corny, and sometimes just perverse. The complaint against Gibson centered on his song "Keep A-Goin,'" performed live in the film at the Grand Ole Opry. Gibson refutes the claim that he stole the song from the litigant. In a detailed explanation, he explains that the song is, in fact, mostly based on the poem of the same name by Frank L. Stanton.[30] As the poem was in the public domain, Gibson was able to use it without clearing copyright. Gibson explains that the plaintiff knew the song from childhood: "It was something she had learned as a kid in school and convinced herself after reciting it all her life that she had written it."[31]

Gibson first recited the poem on an episode of *The Dick Van Dyke Show* ("Talk to the Snail"; aired March 23, 1966). When Altman wanted his actors to work on songs for their characters, Gibson resurrected the already-borrowed Stanton lyrics and made slight revisions. The lyric was then paired with an upbeat musical track by Richard Baskin. Gibson used the first two stanzas of Stanton's poem mostly intact. He replaced the third stanza and wrote a new fourth stanza for the *Nashville* song. Summing up the power of the original Stanton poem, Gibson concludes, "It has endured and may well have nine lives coming after this one. This could only mean that Stanton's original exhortation to persist, to endure, to continue, to Keep A Goin' is being heeded by the work itself."[32] The legal action against Gibson had no merit, yet his usage of the verse does speak to the ways that culture is recycled. From Stanton

HENRY GIBSON

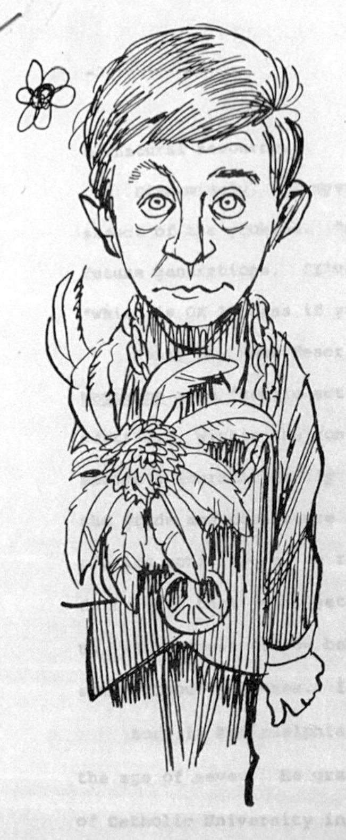

Lots of people are talking about ecology, but very few are doing any-thing about it. One of these few is actor/writer HENRY GIBSON.

When Laugh-In made its explosive debut as a TV special, Henry cap-tivated viewers with his dimpled grin, giant daisy and beguiling poems. And, even before top-rated Laugh-In became a permanent part of the American scene, his quavering "by Henry Gibson" had become a permanent part of the American language.

During his final year as a reg-ular on Laugh-In, people began to notice the change in Henry's weekly poems. They were still absurdly funny, but now more and more of them made us reappraise our environment in terms of pol-lution, overpopulation and the wholesale destruction of

Figure 13: Henry Gibson promotional information.

to *The Dick Van Dyke Show* to *Nashville*, these words illustrate how "the same, but different" defines much of our culture. This kind of reinvention also relates more generally to America, the land in which people can endlessly evolve or remake themselves to chase the American dream.

This maxim applies just as readily to Altman's film overall. Gayle Sherwood Magee's careful examination of the songs in the film reveals that many existed prior to production. Keith Carradine's "I'm Easy" was written while he was appearing in the Broadway musical *Hair*, and "It Don't Worry Me" was inspired by another film of Carradine's, the hobo action drama *Emperor of the North* (1973).[33] As Magee notes, Altman was able to position the music as original for the film and as composed and performed by actors, many with very little previous musical experience.[34] Repurposed music, not composed primarily for the characters and dramatic action of *Nashville*, becomes a marketing asset: "The often repeated belief concerning nonmusical actors writing their own songs from a character's point of view serves as one such example of Altman and his collaborators creating a narrative that would draw attention to the film."[35] Using songs by nonprofessionals was probably also more cost effective than buying the rights to existing and established country songs.[36]

Repurposing is also the central element in another *Nashville* legal issue, the use of Ronee Blakley's songs "My Idaho Home" and "Tapedeck in His Tractor" in her 1975 solo album *Welcome*. The album, scheduled to be released at the end of 1975, foregrounded these two songs in the print ads, reminding potential buyers that Blakley had performed them in *Nash-*

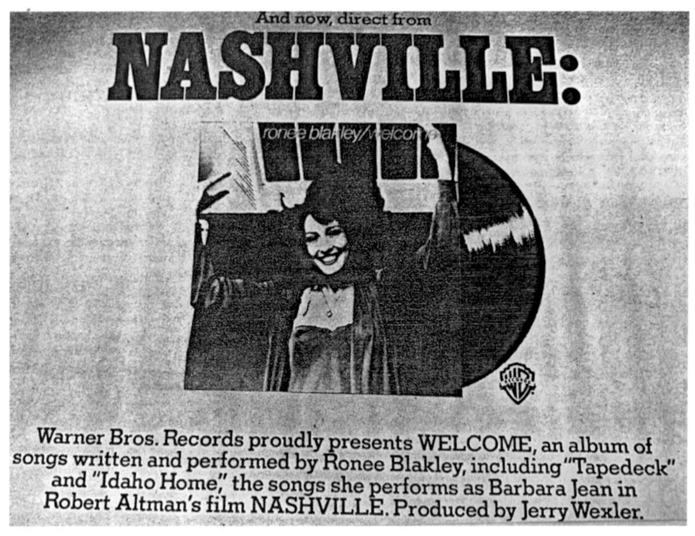

Figure 14: Ronee Blakley record advertisement.

ville. While this strategy could be seen as cross-promotional, benefiting Blakley's album, the *Nashville* soundtrack, and the film, Blakley broke a rerecording restriction in her contract with Altman's company, Landscape Films, that forbade her to record her songs in the film for another label. Both ABC Records (distributor of the soundtrack) and Landscape Films lodged complaints and promised "to take all necessary legal and equitable actions" to protect their rights.[37] In Blakley's defense, the versions of these songs on her album were slightly different, somewhat more in the rock/folk region rather than country music. The case shows how creative reinvention can be curtailed by legal parameters seeking to maintain the economic life of a film and soundtrack album.[38]

The second lesson from the archive speaks to the importance of image management in American culture. Another potential legal entanglement inspires this idea. Harry Birdwell, a former president of the Future Farmers of America (FFA) in a letter to Paramount Pictures, distributor of *Nashville*, expresses his strong disdain for the use of an FFA jacket on Kenny (David Hayward).[39] The FFA is a national organization devoted to advancing careers in agriculture and related industries. Initially Birdwell seems upset by the "wrinkled and filthy quality" of the jacket on screen (this is against the protocols of the FFA). The major complaint, though, is Kenny wearing the jacket when he assassinates Barbara Jean. Noting that the FFA depends on maintaining a positive image, Birdwell asserts that associating the jacket with the moment of violence represents "a tasteless abusive use of the FFA emblem" (the emblem is featured prominently on the back of the jacket).

The complaint, which asks for "a public apology and restitution for damages done," is forwarded from Paramount Pictures to ABC Entertainment and finally to Landscape Films. Lawyers for Landscape Films advise Altman's office to compose a letter of apology stating that there was "no intention to deprecate the organization."[40] Elaine Bradish, Altman's secretary, responds to Birdwell with a note explaining that the jacket was chosen from a thrift store in Nashville; as Bradish comments, "Unfortunately, no one on location was aware of the significance of the insignia or that the jacket was anything more than the right size to fit the actor."[41] Her letter closes with a statement applauding FFA's programs for "fine young

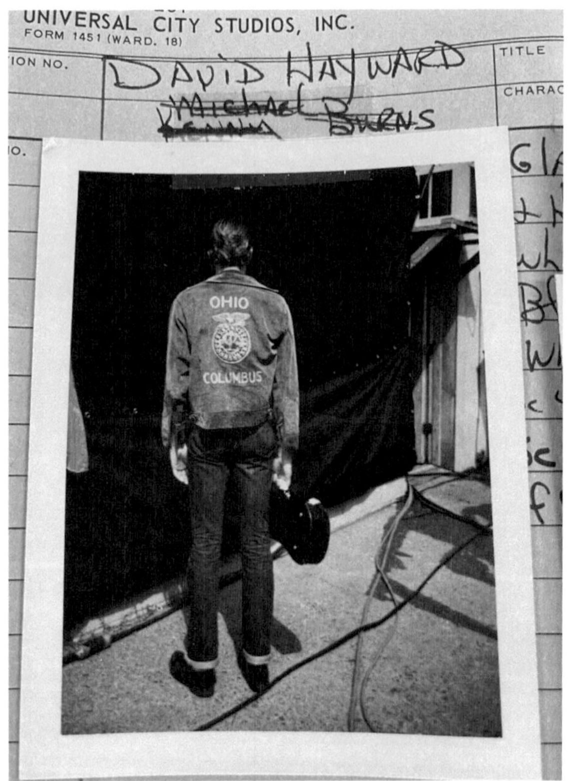

Figure 15: Wardrobe continuity shot of Kenny's jacket.

Americans." The response appears to have appeased Birdwell, and there is no further documentation on the issue.

Keeping in mind the connection between Hal Phillip Walker, farming, and agricultural development, it is possible that the FFA jacket, worn by an assassin with eyes on the candidate, could be a deliberate choice by Altman or a member of his team. Robert Self refers to Altman's ability to capture "subliminal reality," connections in life that are often missed or ignored.[42] Linking Kenny with Hal Phillip Walker through the jacket could easily be an element in Altman's subliminal reality.

The instinct to protect the FFA image was poorly timed (the film had been playing for four months when the complaint appeared). Nothing materialized from the threatened legal action. It is worthwhile noticing that the same FFA jacket is available online at the organization's website, fifty years after *Nashville*'s release. Clearly, the FFA knew then and knows now the value of building and maintaining their image and brand. The larger lesson—being aware of image and how this influences others—is evidenced throughout *Nashville*. Most prominently, the well-defined star images of Haven Hamilton and Barbara Jean are carefully constructed for the public. Haven's squeaky-clean persona establishes him as an unofficial mayor of the city, advocating for family, church, civic pride, and love of country. Private moments reveal that this image does not match the sharp-tongued, angry, calculating figure evident when he is not in the public eye. Barbara Jean's image plays out in a more complicated way: on stage she is clearly authentic, yet in her private life, personal stress, turmoil, and mental illness derail the sunny and positive Barbara Jean known to fans. A compelling star image leads to a closer connection with the fans and, it is hoped, to better record sales and concert attendance.

On a broader level, the film also demonstrates how physical image is central to constructing our own persona, or as sociologist Erving Goffman describes it, our personal front.

Physical typing is important for the film, given the large number of characters. Altman needs each one to be recognizable quickly, given the many fleeting appearances of the ensemble cast. Given her thin physique and tall stature, L.A. Joan makes an impression right away. She also endlessly morphs her physical image through wigs and clothing to match a variety of different social situations. She strives to present herself as physically attractive and trendy, hoping for hookups with stars and access to the best venues. Sueleen also cultivates her image, although less effectively than L.A. Joan. Stuffing gym socks in her bra to increase her bust size, Sueleen's version of visual glamor favors form-fitting and revealing dresses in bright colors. To a lesser extent than the female characters, who are more aware of their status of being on display, men in the film also present physical images that help define their characters, from John Triplette's crisp lightweight blue suit (professional and laid back), the Tricycle Man's huge goggles (countercultural and druggy), and Tom's black T-shirt, tan vest, and jeans (simple, contemporary, and sexy).

The USA of *Nashville*

Extrapolating from Nashville to the country, the overall ideological takeaway from Altman is bleak. America is a country based on the chance to better yourself and to win personal, professional, and financial success. Yet this is mostly an illusion, a fact that people blithely ignore. The American social hierarchy privileges certain groups and excludes others. The chance for those marginalized to attain the American dream

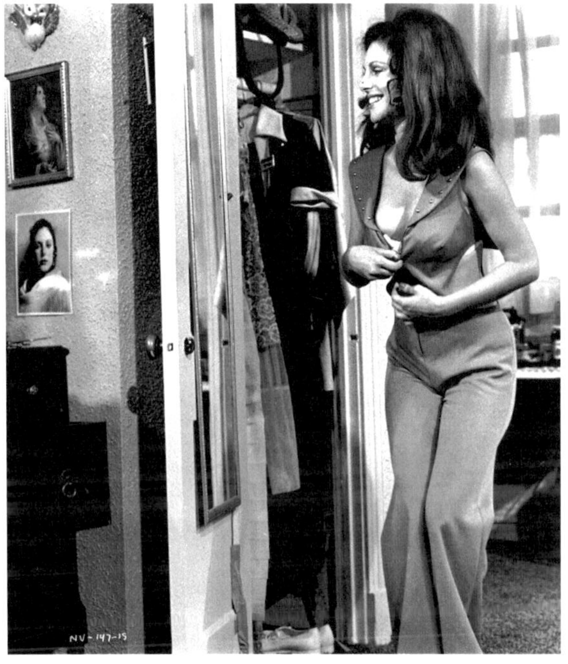

Figure 16: Sueleen (Gwen Welles) pads her bra.

is slim, although most external messaging states just the opposite. Even those who achieve great wealth are still subject to manipulation and control by people seeking to maximize their own financial rewards. A far greater number of people simply try to move up the ladder but are continually thwarted by circumstances and social structures. Following Theodor Adorno and Max Horkheimer's theorizing of the culture industry, popular culture in *Nashville* and the USA lacks authenticity, endlessly recycles content, and is dependent on placing us in set roles that bolster the status quo and the dominant classes. Entertainment placates and pacifies rather than challenges. *Nashville*'s humor and cleverness in design and delivery could be viewed as a means of softening the harsher outlook on American society. The critique can easily be disregarded or glossed over as secondary to the entertainment value of the film.

If this summary is too despairing, it is worth remembering two aspects. First, Altman's flexible design encourages a range of responses, from those taking it at face value to those who see it as a dark satire on America in 1975. Altman's artistry involves walking this fine line so that the content serves multiple purposes and yields a variety of responses, partly based on our backgrounds and political leanings. The second saving grace is a larger, structural one. What does it say about the culture industry and its control when a major studio like Paramount Pictures, then owned by the conglomerate Gulf and Western, distributes a film that is openly critical of the opportunities in American life?[43] In this manner, the culture industry still has room for dissent and contradictions within the entertainment product. Soon enough, with the end of the New Hollywood era, these bright sparks would mostly be extinguished.

CHAPTER 4

Advertising and Marketing Roadblocks

Beginning with Pauline Kael's review of an unfinished *Nashville* several months before its release, *Nashville* was touted as a potential blockbuster. *Variety* summed up these high expectations for commercial success on the film's opening day in New York: "[*Nashville*] has all the earmarks of a major B.O. entry. The pre-opening reception from critics for the Paramount Pictures release has been nothing short of ecstatic, even outdoing the pre-preem reception given Bernardo Bertolucci's *Last Tango in Paris* two and a half years ago."[1] The New York opening was indeed robust: $30,000 at the Baronet theater and $25,000 at Cinema II.[2] This pattern was replicated across several cities: for instance, opening weeks of single engagements of $35,000 in Boston, $34,000 in San Francisco, and $25,000 in Kansas City.[3] Despite these initial grosses and the lofty expectations, the film did not translate to a wide audience. *Nashville*'s release was broadened in the seventh week of release with fair results, but the drop-off happened soon after.[4] *Nashville* made only a modest impact overall at the box office, surprising many critics who predicted the film would be popular.

The commercial success of any film derives from an array of factors, including the textual components of the film, the distribution pattern, the critical reception, publicity, marketing, and advertising. Looking back over half a century, it is impossible to isolate the impact of any *one* factor that softened *Nashville*'s appeal with the public. Nevertheless, an analysis of the film's marketing campaign, from trailer to print ads and posters, helps to illustrate a key framing device for the film, the filter that influenced the film's public reception. In this chapter, I explore essential marketing assets and liabilities of *Nashville*. This project is both evaluative (of the existing marketing collateral) and speculative (of other directions the film might have used to enter the marketplace).

Marketing Benefits and Land Mines

Released in the middle of the New Hollywood period, *Nashville*'s primary marketing asset was Robert Altman. After a lengthy career directing episodic television and a few neglected films (*Countdown*, *That Cold Day in the Park*), Altman was chosen by Twentieth Century-Fox to direct the antiwar black comedy *M*A*S*H*. The film was advertised with a distinctive logo, a peace sign growing into a pair of legs in high heels. The provocative logo was labeled as offensive and sexist in some quarters. The image conveyed the film's irreverence and mischievous quality very clearly. Buoyed also by critical support of, among others, Pauline Kael and Joe Morgenstern, *M*A*S*H* garnered strong box office.[5]

*M*A*S*H* established Altman as a director, and in the New

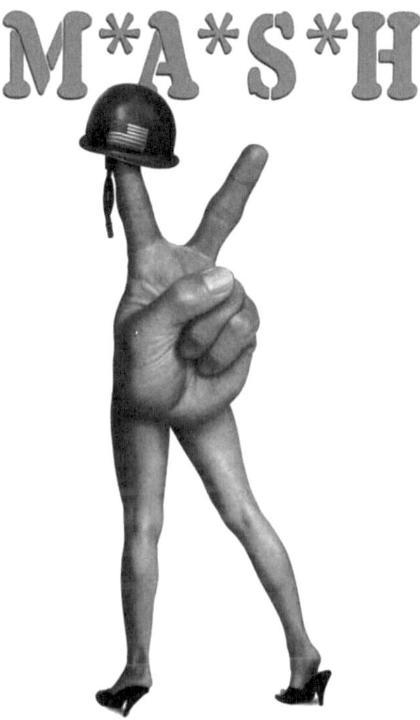

Figure 17: *M*A*S*H* ad logo.

Hollywood era allowed him to be a marker to sell subsequent films. Timothy Corrigan refers to the "commerce of auteurism" as a distinct strategy: "If normally the auteurist text promotes and recuperates a movie, these filmmakers now run the commerce of the auteurist and autonomous self up against its textual expression in a way that shatters the coherence of both authorial expression and stardom."[6] The director becomes a crucial element in building awareness and interest in the film, fueled by interviews along with reviews and advertising mentioning the director. This tendency can be seen with the campaign for *Brewster McCloud*, Altman's follow-up to *M*A*S*H*, a quirky fable about a disillusioned young man building human "wings" so he can fly in the Houston Astrodome. Whimsical and soaked in the counterculture of the time, *Brewster McCloud* was released by MGM with the tagline "'Something else' from the director of *M*A*S*H*." This approach foregrounds the director but yields little other information or any compelling marketing angles ("something else" feels like an indifferent way to position the film). Clearly not an exploitation film, like other contemporary easy-to-market MGM releases of that era such as *Shaft* (1971) and *Kansas City Bomber* (1972), the film's distributor was not ready to handle the challenge of selling *Brewster McCloud* beyond highlighting the auteurist angle (Altman even appears in the film's poster along with the cast members). Lacking the antiwar commentary and sharp humor of *M*A*S*H*, *Brewster McCloud* was a dismal commercial failure on release, grossing slightly less than $1 million domestically.[7]

The strategy of foregrounding Altman as the key selling point is evidenced throughout the early 1970s: Columbia referred to Robert Altman's *Images* in the advertising for that film, and, echoing the *Brewster McCloud* imagery, Altman directly appeared in *The Long Goodbye* poster designed by *Mad* magazine illustrator Jack Davis.[8] Critical support also bolstered Altman's image and became a key auxiliary method to sell his films. Understanding that the New Hollywood period privileged critical response as part of the deep investment in film culture, critics advocated for the director in reviews and in public appearances. Pauline Kael, for instance, appeared on *The Dick Cavett Show* to complain that other critics had unfairly dismissed *McCabe & Mrs. Miller*. She had made an impassioned plea for Altman's creative vision and argued that the film needed to stay in theaters so that audiences could discover it. Sometimes critical acclaim for the director and one of his films became the sole means of advertising. For *McCabe & Mrs. Miller*'s New York opening, entire reviews by Judith Crist (*New York* magazine) and Pauline Kael (*New Yorker*) were reprinted and used as newspaper ads.

Beyond Altman, the marketing benefits of *Nashville* were much less obvious. The large cast, rather than being an asset, represented a challenge to selling the film. The number of actors in Altman's film is daunting. Second, the *Nashville* cast was primarily newcomers (e.g., Ronee Blakley, David Hayward, Scott Glenn), character actors (e.g., Keenan Wynn, Barbara Baxley, Ned Beatty), and Altman ensemble players (e.g., Shelley Duvall, Keith Carradine, Bert Remsen). Only three actors could be considered to fall outside these parameters: Lily Tomlin, Henry Gibson, and Karen Black.

Lily Tomlin and Henry Gibson both appeared in the topical sketch comedy and variety show *Laugh-In*. Airing from 1968 through 1973, the show covered a barrage of contemporary issues, from civil rights to feminism and disillusionment with the American political scene. Tomlin essayed regular characters such as Ernestine, the adenoidal telephone operator, the precocious five-year-old Edith Ann, and the ever-so-proper Tasteful Lady. Gibson, as mentioned previously, gained notoriety for his emotionally flat poetry readings on the show.

After the show finished, Tomlin began appearing in her own television variety specials and continued to record successful comedy albums.[9] Gibson made numerous guest TV show appearances and, notably, played against type as a manipulative and evil doctor in Altman's *The Long Goodbye*. Gibson and especially Tomlin had some public recognition, much more than others in the *Nashville* cast. Accordingly, Altman used the appearance of Tomlin and Gibson to lure audiences to attend *Nashville*'s Grand Ole Opry musical scenes. While they probably had some name recognition, neither Tomlin nor Gibson would be sufficient as a marketing the film. If *Nashville* had been a broader satire in line with *Laugh-In*, then this approach might have been more viable. As is, the film features Tomlin in a dramatic role far from her signature comic characters, a transition that could have been off-putting for her fans.

A true emblem of the New Hollywood cinema, Karen Black appeared in seminal films from the period, including *Easy Rider* (1969), *Drive, He Said* (1971), and, in a heartbreaking Oscar-nominated performance, as the vulnerable waitress Rayette in *Five Easy Pieces* (1970). Black's offbeat looks and intensity proved to be too much for Hollywood to cast her in leading roles. During the period leading to *Nashville*, she largely appeared as part of an ensemble cast (*Airport 75* [1974], *The Outfit* [1973]), in fringe independent movies (*The Pyx* [1973], *Rhinoceros* [1974]), or in juicy supporting roles, such as the other woman Myrtle in *The Great Gatsby* (1974). Her most prominent leading role, as Faye in *The Day of the Locust* (1975), was impacted by the film's dismal public and critical reception. Black's performance was bold and uncompromising; she refused to make the character

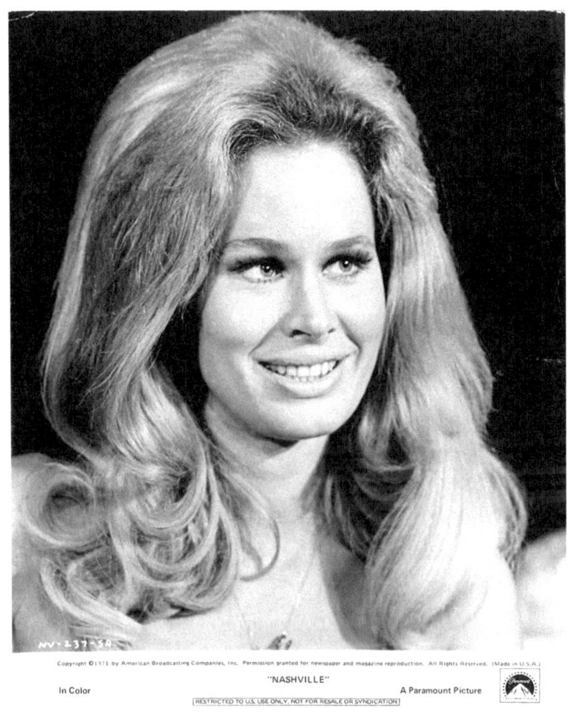

Figure 18: Karen Black appears as country star Connie White.

sympathetic and was unafraid of appearing foolish or mean-spirited. With Connie White's limited screen time and Black's sharp-edged performance, Black seemed unlikely to be a marketing focus for the film. *Nashville* would not prove to be her breakthrough role.[10]

The rise of country music and crossovers with folk and pop in the 1970s could also be leveraged as an appeal for the film. Recall that executive producer Jerry Weintraub had a considerable background in the agency business, representing many music stars, from Frank Sinatra to John Denver. *Nashville* was Weintraub's first venture into filmmaking, and the musical connection could have been an impetus for his involvement. Weintraub sold the film to ABC Entertainment, who hoped to reap profits from the ABC Records soundtrack album and from eventual television airings on the ABC Network.[11] Pinning the commercial fate of the film on the music and soundtrack album was never a feasible option, though. As Altman commented on the liner notes to the MCA *Nashville* album reissue from 2000, "We weren't trying to write 'great' songs. We aimed to meet the spectrum of songs coming out of the Nashville scene." This caveat illustrates Altman's knowledge that the soundtrack was a curious blend of obviously bad, comic, and corny songs (e.g., the Henry Gibson numbers), light folk/pop songs (Keith Carradine), middling country ballads (Karen Black, Timothy Brown), and solid up-tempo and emotional country songs (Ronee Blakley). Musical director Richard Baskin smartly bolstered the score by hiring seasoned local session players such as Vassar Clements and Weldon Myrick. Just as a listening experience, divorced from the film, the soundtrack makes broad tonal shifts from sanctimonious and comical "For the Sake of the Children" to the heartfelt "My Idaho Home." The soundtrack does not coalesce as a country or pop album and would make sense mainly to those who have seen the film. For multiple reasons, the music by itself would be a difficult angle to sell the film.

The positioning of *Nashville* in the media marketplace was also influenced by the curious space offered by rural and Southern culture. Mixed messages were being sent by the media industries. In a sweeping move, CBS cancelled its slate of popular "rural comedies," including *The Beverly Hillbillies* and *Green Acres*, both placing in Nielsen's Top 20 programs, to make way for more realistic depictions of urban and suburban life. As David Marc notes, the move could have been motivated by more discrete Nielsen ratings identifying the value of a younger eighteen-to-thirty-four- demographic, which the rural comedies failed to reach.[12] The southern, rural market was certainly represented, though, by "Nashville's answer to *Laugh-In*" (to invoke Hal Erickson's description), the comedy and country music syndicated show *Hee Haw*.[13] Reinforcing many Southern stereotypes and set in a cornfield, the show was dismissed by critics but embraced by audiences (it ran for twenty-four years, until 1993). Cohost Roy Clark explained its appeal to multiple audiences: "Anybody can grasp this material. Sophisticated people see the show as a tremendous put-on and satire; and country people take it right at face value."[14] Keep in mind that the satire of *Hee Haw* was populated with country stars, comedians, and the buxom Hee Haw Honeys, giving the show an authenticity that differentiated it from Altman's more high-minded satirical take on country music culture. Did the presence of *Hee Haw* make country fans feel that they already had their satire and comedy and make them suspicious of anything claiming to offer the same?

Evaluating *Nashville*'s Marketing and Advertising

The Press Kit and Trailer

Keeping these potential marketing assets in mind, an examination of *Nashville*'s advertising reveals how Paramount Pictures struggled to find a place for the film with a broad audience. Before analyzing the print ads, trailer, and other ads, the films' press kit, or "Handbook of Production Information," presents several ways the distributor thought the film would appeal to potential viewers. A press kit of the period was comprised of basic production information, bios for the cast and creative talent, and short stories highlighting different aspects of the film. These stories would typically be a jumping-off point for a journalists' own piece on the film (although occasionally lazy journalists would just use chunks of the provided press kit story as their own).

In addition to a full set of credits, a narrative synopsis, and cast bios, Paramount Pictures supplied six discrete stories, each highlighting a marketable element of *Nashville*. As would be expected, the auteurist angle described Altman's style as capturing events "as they happen." *Nashville* was tagged as "the ultimate Altman movie," with the story highlighting Altman's ability to integrate documentary filming with narrative cinema. The article locates Altman's auteurism in "a multiplicity of characters and events," matched with a "free-wheeling narrative style." Ample quotes from the director are used to explain his methods and decision-making.

The remaining five stories/positionings for the film highlighted the female actors (Lily Tomlin, Barbara Harris, Gwen

Welles, Karen Black, and Ronee Blakley). There are no stories on the male actors. Perhaps this decision was made to respond to the charges of sexism leveled at Altman for his male-oriented films, such as *M*A*S*H* or *California Split*. Each story centers on a unique perspective the actor brought to the project. Lily Tomlin's profile leads with her memorable characters from *Laugh-In* and then emphasizes her transition from a comedic to dramatic actress in the film. Barbara Harris's roots in improvisation are tied to Altman's own commitment to realism and authenticity. Breaking from the other stories, Gwen Welles's profile prominently mentions her three *Playboy* pictorials and that magazine's describing her as "the best copy since Marilyn Monroe." Karen Black, described as playing "all of the coveted female leads in Hollywood," is praised for bringing her singing ability to the screen for the first time. Ronee Blakley has the strongest pitch. Comparing her to an unknown Lana Turner being discovered in a drugstore, the writer enthuses that "Ronee proves the dream factory is alive and well . . . and thriving." Clearly the Paramount marketers considered her to be a possible breakthrough star. This confidence was met with critical praise for her performance as well as multiple publicity opportunities, including Blakley on the cover of *Newsweek* and in a featured story in *People* magazine.

In 1975, the primary means for advertising a new film were a trailer, one or more posters, newspaper ads, and sometimes television commercials. The Paramount trailer for *Nashville* does not focus either on Altman or on any of the female actors featured in the press kit stories. The trailer attempts the impossible: to detail each of the twenty-four characters and their relationships in only two minutes. Breathlessly, a narrator begins by telling us the film covers "five days in the lives of twenty-four unforgettable people." He then proclaims, "That's a lot of characters so listen carefully!" The stern call to action almost suggests that the viewer will get a pop quiz at the end. The trailer rushes through a brief description of each character, usually linked to their function in the film.

This marketing approach presents many problems. Viewers get exhausted trying to understand the array of characters, and the trailer fails to explain why we should care about each person and their situation. The narration links duos (e.g., Mr. Green–L.A. Joan) or trios (e.g., Tom, Bill, and Mary), but fails to address how the characters intertwine and why these connections are important to the film. As a result, the trailer misrepresents *Nashville* as a series of separate stories that apparently are not joined in any way. Further, in trying to entice viewers, the narration gives away far too much of the developing dramatic action. Consider this introduction, which fully reveals the character's drama and decision-making: "Lily Tomlin is a gospel singer who strays just a little when she has a one-night stand with Keith Carradine, a hot young rock singer." In the most egregious lapse, David Hayward's assassin Kenny is described as "a sensitive boy who has a big surprise in store for everyone." The trailer completely omits the connecting story of the Hal Phillip Walker political rally that eventually brings together the whole cast. Without this thread, the daunting list of cast members becomes even more confusing. Apart from their direct connection to one or two others, the characters seem to exist in isolation. Forgetting the most marketable element, director Altman is hardly mentioned as well.

The Print Ad: Poster and Newspaper Ads

The one-sheet for *Nashville* featured a microphone, with shapely legs and high heels, holding an American flag top hat. Fireworks explode in the background of the ad. The tagline at the top of the poster proclaims "The damndest thing you ever saw." The poster is clearly inspired by the iconic image used to sell *M*A*S*H*, a hand with fingers on high heels, two other fingers giving a peace sign, and a military helmet featuring an American flag dangling from a finger. The high heels, legs, and American flag hat all reappear in the *Nashville* poster. The association with *M*A*S*H* given the similarity in images is lessened by the gap of five years between the films. The *M*A*S*H* image connotes sexiness, rebellion, and the counterculture; *Nashville*'s picture conveys much less. The legs on the microphone and the American hat might suggest a patriotic singing and dancing musical. In this context, the fireworks indicate a July 4th celebration. This reading is, of course, distant from the content of the film. The southern, country-and-western associations are not addressed by the image at all.[15]

For the first-release wave (June–July 1975), the microphone logo with critical quotes was used in many cities (including Boston, Chicago, Detroit, Indianapolis, Memphis, San Francisco, and Toronto). The New York newspaper advertising varied slightly and was composed primarily of ecstatic critics' quotes (e.g., "'A pageant of celebration!'—Vincent Canby,

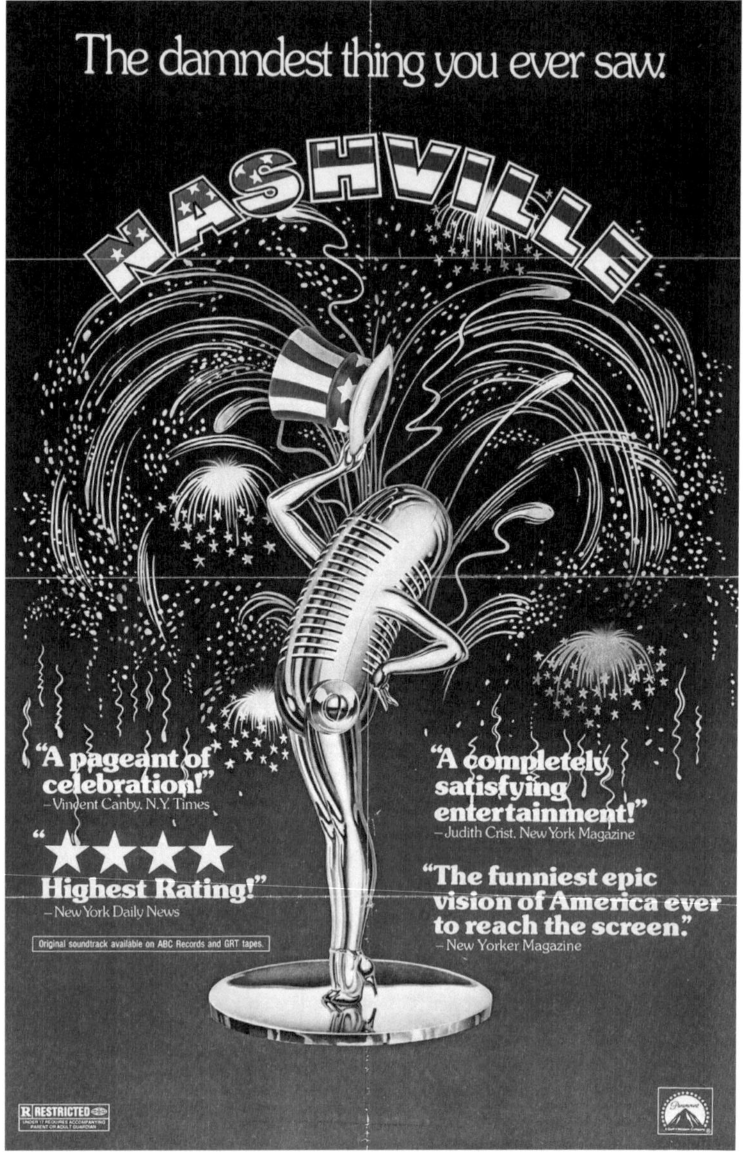

Figure 19: Dancing microphone poster ad.

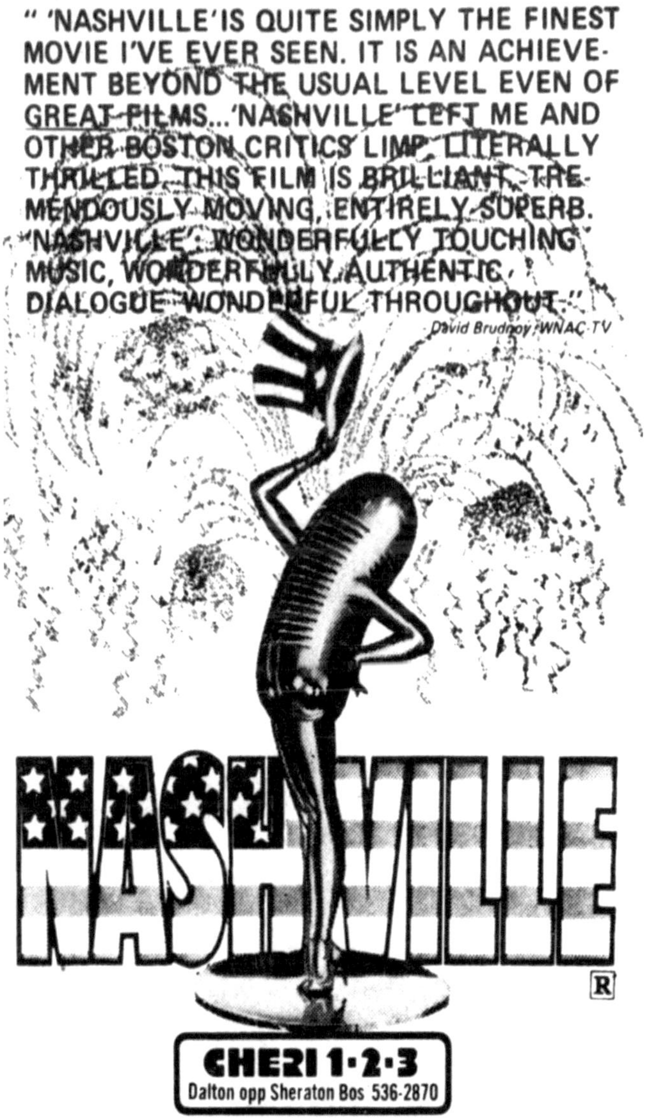

Figure 20: Microphone newspaper ad.

New York Times"). The New York papers also utilized a new title treatment with the American flag superimposed on the letters of the word "Nashville." While favorable critical opinion was included in many markets, in New York, very positive quotes eclipsed all the other visual elements in print advertising.

As the film played in more markets, Paramount transitioned to a new marketing campaign.[16] The microphone was replaced with the back of a large sequined jean jacket with small images of all twenty-four cast members. The person wearing the jacket holds a license plate with the film's title.[17] The text in the ad alternated between two options: (1) "Wild. Wonderful. Sinful. Laughing. Explosive," and (2) "One. It's a story of lovers and laughers and losers and winners. Two. It's about 5 days in the lives of 24 people. Three. It's the damndest movie entertainment you ever saw. Go. See it! Everybody is!" Switching advertising images and taglines after a film's opening is risky; efforts to build an image for the film initially are either undone or revised in a crowded marketplace for viewer attention.

The jean-jacket image recalls a discarded advertising sketch by Richard Amsel, who made the initial poster for *The Long Goodbye* and the final poster for *McCabe & Mrs. Miller*. Amsel, the most famous film graphic poster designer of the 1970s, best known for his iconic *Raiders of the Lost Ark* (1981) one-sheet, completed an impressive, but unused, poster for *Nashville*: a suede fringed shirt with the arm composed of small stars, each displaying an image of a cast member. The figure in the poster holds a microphone with the cord spelling the film's title and ending with a spark. The stars/pictures in

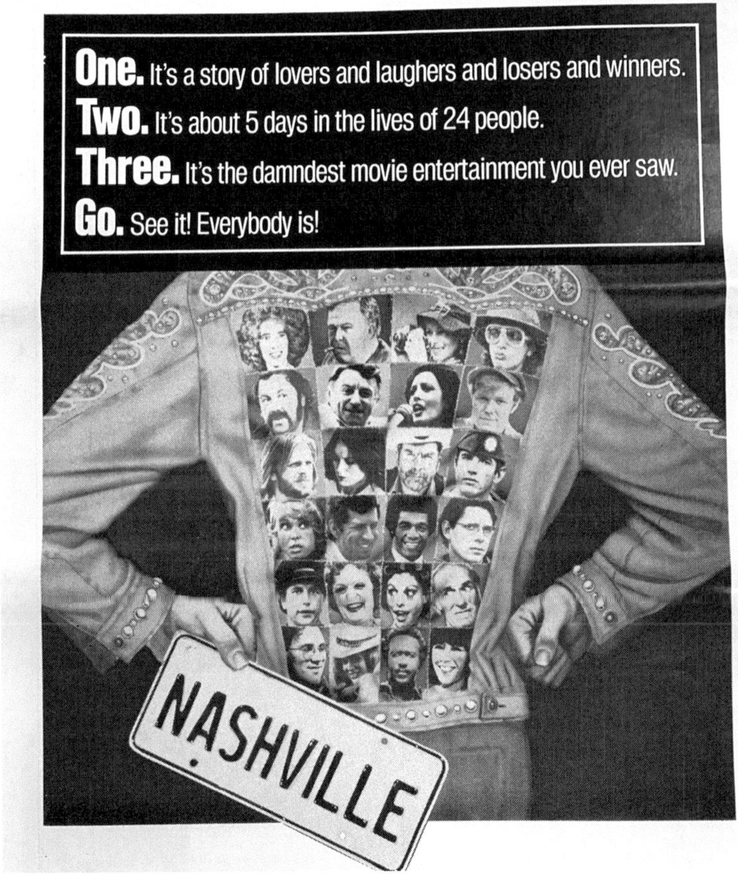

One. It's a story of lovers and laughers and losers and winners.
Two. It's about 5 days in the lives of 24 people.
Three. It's the damndest movie entertainment you ever saw.
Go. See it! Everybody is!

NASHVILLE

Figure 21: Jean jacket poster ad.

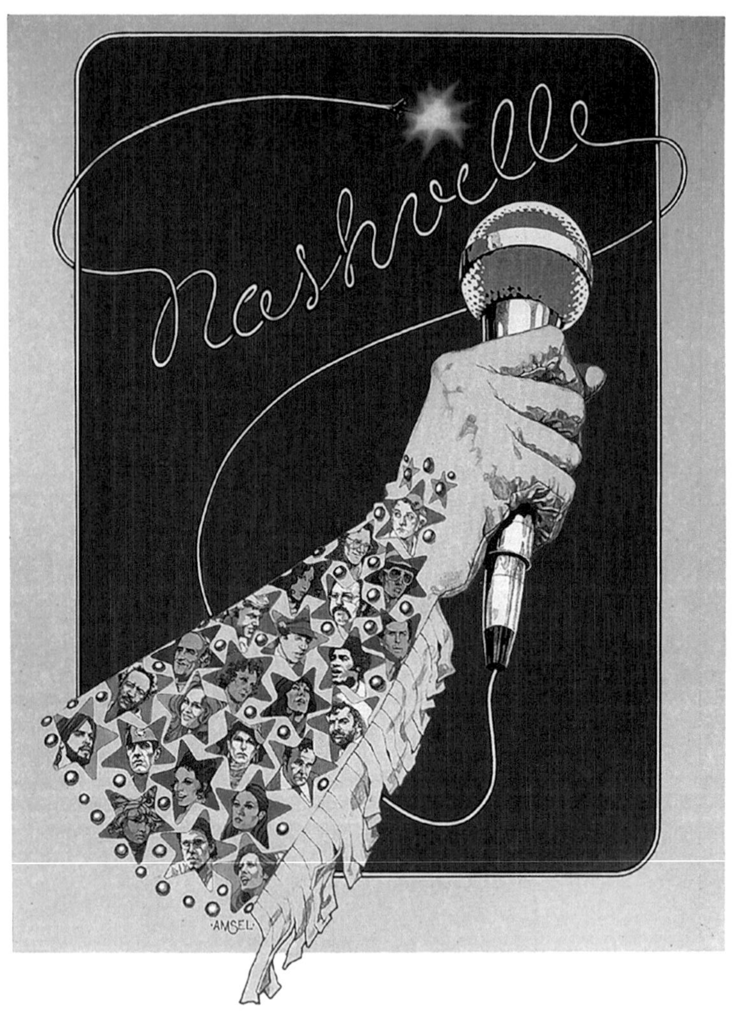

Figure 22: Unused Richard Amsel *Nashville* poster.

Amsel's design are echoed in the jean-jacket head shots. Altman rejected other designs for being too polished, and this was probably the issue with Amsel's poster. Altman described the city of Nashville as a "run down, garish, raunchy place" and wanted the artwork for the film to reflect this.[18]

This revised jean-jacket print campaign minimized the critical quotes, using the new taglines in their place. As the film entered more markets, Paramount possibly thought that viewers in the suburban and rural markets valued critical reviews less than viewers in the larger cities. If that was the case, the creative advertising takes on even greater importance as a crucial marketing element. It is also possible that the dancing microphone simply did not convey the film adequately or create strong want-to-see interest among potential audience members.

The jean-jacket ad, somewhat ineffectively, sought to address these deficiencies. The large cast was represented visually, although each person was difficult to identify given the small size of the individual headshots (this was exacerbated as the newspaper ads shrank in size over the weeks). Most (all?) of the cast cannot be identified in these tiny pictures, so the effect of the jacket is simply of a cross-section of people. With the title *Nashville* on the license plate, the film could then be misinterpreted as a documentary on the town or the country music scene. Neither tagline solved the issue of the tough-to-decipher jean jacket. "Wild. Wonderful. Sinful. Laughing. Explosive" is a set of highly passionate words but, without an adequate narrative context, they fail to coalesce into a brand promise from the film. The second numbered tagline is a little more grounded: the first two bullets specify the time frame and the large cast and vague comedic and dramatic stakes. The third bullet borrows the problematic "damndest" tagline. The final bullet ("See it! Everyone is!") reeks of desperation and a complete lack of invention. Rather than build from broader to specific reasons to see *Nashville*, the tagline simply falls apart; the numbering feels like an unneeded element as well.

The jean-jacket campaign did not facilitate the move to smaller markets in the late summer and the fall. Despite critical acclaim, Paramount appears to have lost interest in marketing the film by the end of the year. The film even received a Best Picture Academy Award nomination, but it was not rereleased to take advantage of this honor.

The J. William Myers Alternative

Nashville artist William Myers tagged along during the film's production, supposedly on assignment for the *Los Angeles Times*. Myers was able to sketch accurate and memorable caricatures of each actor. Myer's artwork places all twenty-four cartoon characters against the Parthenon, with characters grouped by their connection to each other. In a clever move, Myers also sets characters adjacent to each other if they eventually connect through the narrative. For instance, Tom's hand nearly touches Linnea's shoulder. Albuquerque and husband Star, estranged and separated for most of the action, are pictured on opposite sides, connected by an eyeline match and Star's fist raised in anger at his wife. The faces are detailed and

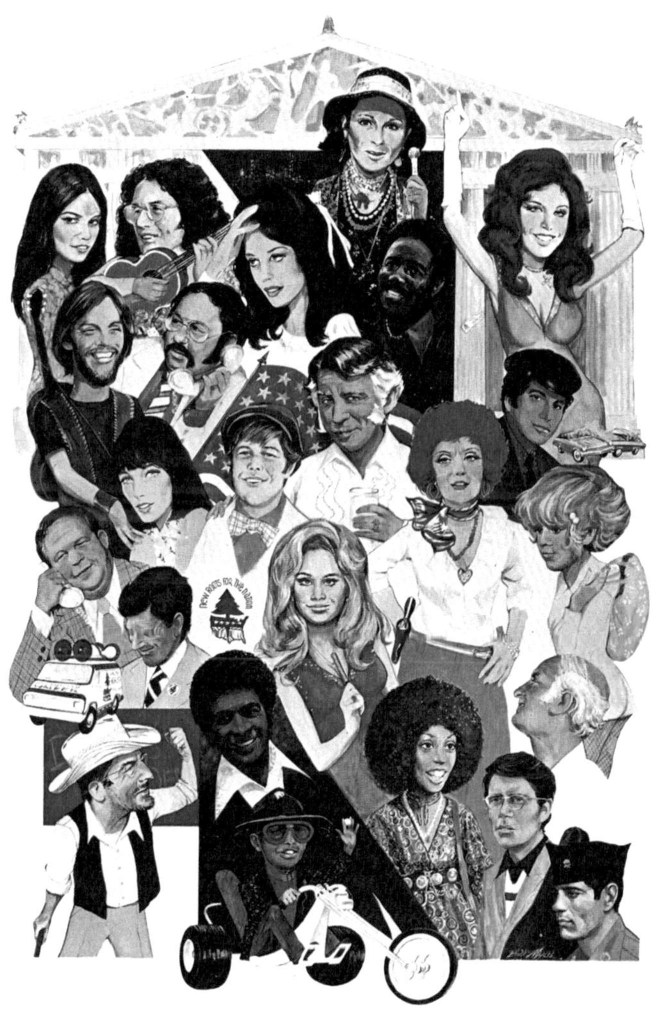

Figure 23: J. William Myers's *Nashville* artwork.

full of feeling and the physical dimension of each character is portrayed nicely. Details include the car crash, the Hal Philip Walker van, the Hal Phillip Walker "New Roots for the Nation" logo, and a large American flag. Myers's artwork captures Altman's film—the large cast, the relationships, and even the color scheme (red, white, and blue). The cartoon images give a levity to the film that the jean jacket and even the dancing microphone could not achieve. The picture is professional without being too glossy or polished (like the Amsel *Nashville* image).

The stills archive at Paramount Pictures contains earlier iterations of the Myers poster. The differences are small but revealing: Opal is smiling more broadly, Connie White looks somewhat menacing and villainous, and Linnea, now radiantly happy, is no longer positioned as closely to Tom. In the finished Myers poster, Opal becomes a more neutral figure, Connie White looks professional and inviting, and Linnea is modest and more pivoted toward Tom. All these changes fit with the characters' portrayal in the completed film.

Altman attempted to develop an ad campaign with general appeal. As he stated to journalist Joseph Gelmis, "I am trying to get tacky with the ad campaign to keep *Nashville* from being a film for the intelligentsia. We've already got them. Now we beat the bushes for the others."[19] Altman requested that the Myers image be used for the poster, but he was rejected by Paramount, who favored the dancing microphone.[20] Alan Rudolph recalls that the Myers image was Altman's favorite among all the possibilities.[21] Altman was able to use this image on the soundtrack album cover and on the published screenplay from Bantam Books.[22]

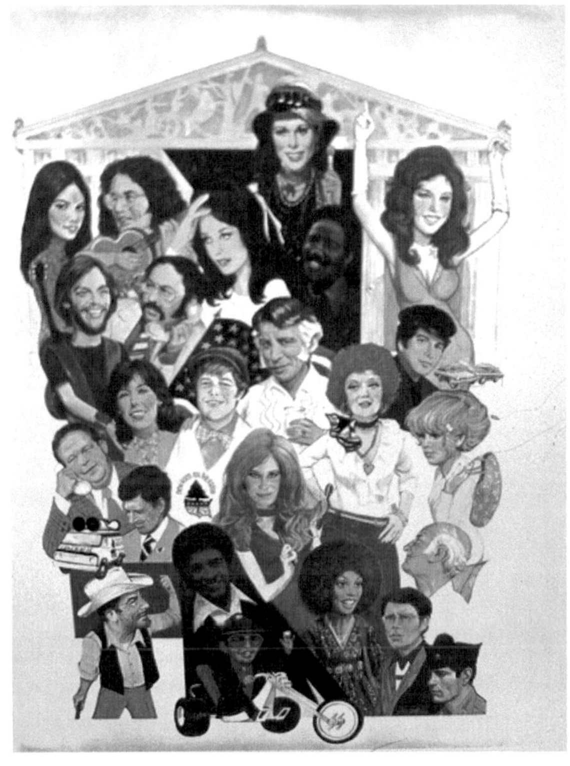

Figure 24: Variation of J. William Myers's *Nashville* artwork.

Arguably the most striking appearance of the Myers artwork is the *Nashville* titles sequence designed by Dan Perri. The titles sequence began as Perri's TV commercial for the film, but Altman adopted it for the main title sequence as well. Using the Myers poster as his basis, Perri constructed a hard-selling barker pushing the *Nashville* actors. As the pitch

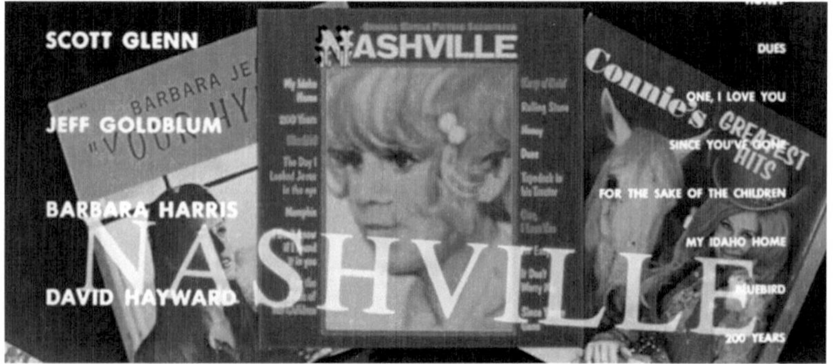

Figure 25: *Nashville* titles sequence designed by Dan Perri.

is made, titles and song sheets of hits from the fictional singers rotate on both sides of the screen. Perri based his titles on late-night rock-and-roll music collection commercials for K-Tel Records. Perri describes his process in these terms: "The announcer screamed the virtues of the music as it blasted out at you with ten different things spinning and flashing loudly at the same time. So, I wrote a 60-second commercial to sell *Nashville* to TV viewers. I found Johnny Grant, the announcer of the K-Tel Records ads and hired him to scream the virtues of the movie. It worked perfectly."[23]

Perri's creation with Myers's artwork at the center is perhaps the golden ticket for selling *Nashville*. The titles are satirical, funny, silly, and in-your-face. The K-Tel television commercials were well known and somewhat despised, so Perri's *Nashville* version lampoons that target as well. Most significantly, while all the stars are mentioned, it is impossible to recall everyone, given the speedy barker's pitch. An audience member instead internalizes the tone/mood (fast-paced) and the country music theme and location. The biggest takeaway is that the titles encapsulate a sense of fun and adventure for viewers about to discover Altman's take on the country town.

The titles fit perfectly with the Robin Wood model of "smart-ass and cutie-pie" that is characteristic of Altman's work.[24] Wood sees Altman's artistry as being antagonistic (sharp, cutting satire, with a mean edge) and disarming (fun, sweet-natured). The combination of smart-ass and cutie-pie is evident in moments of humor in Altman's films. The Perri titles with the K-Tel commercial framework is clever, inventive, and slightly over the top. The humor is both piercing and playful. If only Paramount had pursued this for their advertising efforts, the film might have garnered a larger audience.

Remember that the Myers artwork and Perri creations were not part of Paramount's marketing tool kit for the film.[25] The distributor relied on the dancing microphone and jean-jacket ads as the primary mechanisms to boost awareness of and interest in the film. The campaign tried to position the film as being about everyone, and, most audaciously, about everything. With such a diffused approach, potential viewers were probably left confused and unsure about the film's plot. Placing aside other factors, *Nashville* must be seen as a missed messaging and marketing opportunity.

The Consequences of *Nashville*'s Advertising Failure

Could *Nashville* have been saved commercially by a different advertising strategy? If Paramount had embraced the

Myers image and the Perri titles as a focus, it would have foregrounded the humor of the film. This might have made the film more inviting for potential viewers. Alternately, Paramount could have followed through on one of their marketing angles from the press kit. Highlighting Ronee Blakley in a breakthrough performance or the set of female actors working together might have yielded additional interest. Instead, Paramount had to contend with shifting advertising images, neither of which communicated the substance or tone of the film in a meaningful way. No doubt the film's length and R rating were also detriments for some viewers.[26]

Claiming auteur status is a double-edged sword: a success gets attributed mainly to the director, but so does a failure, or in *Nashville*'s case, a commercial disappointment. The narrative of Altman as an uncommercial director was strengthened by *Nashville*'s soft box office. Several articles, including the *Newsweek* cover story, mentioned that Altman's films had underperformed financially after the commercial success of *M*A*S*H*.[27] *Nashville* was expected to be a blockbuster; Pauline Kael proclaimed, "This picture is going to take off into the stratosphere." Journalist Ray McClain concurred with Kael's sentiment, stating that *Nashville* has reestablished Altman's "commercial reputation as a bankable director."[28] When *Nashville* stalled at the box office, the conventional wisdom was that the film played well in urban centers but could not gain traction in the suburbs or rural areas. Industry analyst Stuart Byron summed up the film's performance in these terms: "*Nashville* cost only $2,200,000 and is thus probably some $1,200,000 into a profit situation, but it is still amazing to me that the impression was so prevalent in the cultural reaches of Manhattan that *Nashville* was one of the year's commercial blockbusters rather than, as it was, the twenty-seventh highest-grossing film of the year."[29]

This underwhelming result was followed by the pathetic gross of *Buffalo Bill and the Indians, or Sitting Bull's History Lesson*. Budgeted at $6 million, the film made less than a million ($869,569 total gross). *Buffalo Bill* producer Dino DeLaurentiis dropped Altman from *Ragtime* (1981), the adaptation of the E. L. Doctorow novel piecing together New York life at the turn of the twentieth century. Between *Nashville* and *Buffalo Bill*, Altman became a filmmaker without a connection to the mass public. Ironically, despite a respectable gross ($60 million worldwide), Altman's *Popeye* (1980) was widely perceived as a relative commercial failure. Was this perception filtered through the image of Altman as an uncommercial auteur? Additionally, *Popeye* was hampered by inflated expectations for a pre-sold cartoon property coming to film.

The other outcome of the failed messaging and public indifference to *Nashville* is the belief that the film is inaccessible, loved mainly by critics and the cultural intelligentsia rather than everyday people. This framing leads to *Nashville* most often being characterized in conceptual terms as a statement on America. What's missing from this focus is the levity and entertainment value in the film.[30] *Nashville* continually slips between different strains of humor: physical farce (the car crashes, the destroyed parking lot guardrail), the overblown comic tunes (especially the Haven Hamilton numbers), snide and sarcastic comments (Connie White dissing Julie Christie), off-kilter social observations (Opal's musings on American culture, the jokes around race), and the bizarre, idiosyncratic Hal Phillip Walker talking points (Christmas smelling like oranges, Columbus's voyage vs. the cost of an automobile). These moments are placed within a satirical context. The humor is balanced by those storylines with an emotional and dramatic bent, such as Barbara Jean's struggles with mental health or Sueleen's relentless efforts to ignore those exploiting her. The result is a film that has broader entertainment appeal than would be apparent from reading the critical reviews.

Seventeen years later, Altman's comeback film *The Player* (1992) was launched with a campaign that embraced the smart-ass and cutie-pie selling approach and strong reliance on comedy and entertainment value. Fine Line Features emphasized the humor over the thriller aspects of studio executive Griffin Mill's deadly encounter with a disgruntled screenwriter. The poster's logo captured the black comedy perfectly: a large noose made of celluloid in which Griffin sways jauntily while chatting on his cell phone. Unlike the *Nashville* dancing microphone, *The Player* logo offers a taste of the thrills, narrative context, and, most of all, the humor in Altman's film. Selling an Altman film should take into account the comic sensibility and sharp humor of the director, both so evident in *Nashville*.

CHAPTER 5

The Mysteries on the Contact Sheets

This chapter focuses on a very specific element connected to the film: black-and-white and color still images created during production. Some images became part of the film's publicity and marketing campaign developed by Paramount Pictures. But many other images, used for wardrobe, continuity, and behind-the-scenes coverage, are part of Altman's archive and have never before been available to the public.[1] I am interested in how the *Nashville* still images affect our understanding of the film's narrative and development. As a key film in the New Hollywood era, *Nashville* has been the focus of much textual analysis celebrating Altman's documentary-like style and the jagged little personal stories and insights of the large cast of characters. The film text does not live in a vacuum, however. Allied materials and artifacts, such as these stills, influence how we process the film, acting as guides or filters to the primary text. In this way, looking at the stills allows us to think about a contextual analysis of the film, multiplying the potential meanings from Altman's film. The archival images also illuminate aspects of Altman's filmmaking, particularly which characters and scenes were omitted from the final cut and how these decisions shaped the film and its design. The stills become a means to break open the film text and to consider alternate directions for the film and its reception. In this way, this project is speculative, designed to problematize accepted readings of the characters, their relationships, and the narrative.

Comprehending the Film Still

Before exploring the *Nashville* artifacts, it is worth recalling different approaches to analyzing film stills. Roland Barthes's "The Third Meaning" addresses this issue directly. Beginning with a still from Eisenstein's *Ivan the Terrible* (1945), Barthes argues that a film still is based on elements "inside the shot" rather than those "between the shots" in a motion picture. The *Ivan the Terrible* image of two courtiers pouring gold over a young czar's head has both an informational and a symbolic level.[2] While the informational level accounts for the basic action, setting, and characters, the symbolic notions of wealth and privilege are denoted by the baptism of gold. Far more slippery is the "third meaning," the obtuse, erratic, or obstinate, as Barthes describes it. Focusing on the appearance, makeup, and expression of the two courtiers, Barthes constructs an elaborate explanation of how each courtier is defined. In doing so, Barthes readily admits that this meaning is particular: "Something in the two faces exceeds psychology, anecdote, function, exceeds meaning without, however, coming down to the obstinacy in presence shown by any human body."[3] Philip Watts sums up this level of interpretation: "What strikes Barthes is affect, the emotion produced by the insignificant detail, the trivial object, the commonplace element that somehow seems slightly out of place."[4] Another way to think of Barthes's third meaning is as connotation, which may vary considerably given the individual reader/viewer, whereas the denotation is more straightforward (and akin to Barthes's first level of meaning). This distinction is crucial for understanding why even a single image yields many different and at times contradictory readings.

Still Life, a book edited by Diane Keaton and Marvin Heiferman, richly demonstrates how film stills have a life far beyond their connection to the individual film. The images range from the classical Hollywood period through the 1960s and are distinguished by glossy photos evoking a strong mood or emotion. Heiferman describes how each image creates meaning, often separate from the film: "Each photograph is a punchline, cut off from its narrative mooring. Each is a photodrama, the distillation of artifice, ideas, assumptions, and evidence. Each is a proclamation and a promise."[5] So, as the editors describe, the still images are so dramatic that they inspire each viewer to create their own potential story from the image, which may in fact have little or no connection to the cinematic narrative. A still from *Bigger than Life* (1956) presents James Mason looming over a frustrated young boy while a mother stands rigidly at the back of the room. As Keaton describes the image, "Without having seen the film, you couldn't possibly have any idea what's going on. You would make up your own story based on who you are and what you see."[6] Through its juxtaposition of over sixty photos, *Still Life* illustrates the separation of the single image from the film and the ways that just one image can create its own narrative.

While some *Nashville* images are single shots, many of the archived photographs are part of contact sheets. Karina Longworth offers a valuable definition of the contact sheet: "A contact sheet—also known as a proof sheet or contact print—is a printed reproduction of one or more strips of developed film, exposed at a one-to-one ratio in order to produce positive images in the same size as the frames on the negative."[7] Unlike the individual still, the contact sheet depends on the shot-to-shot connection. In this way, the contact sheet hews more closely to the experience of watching a scene or sequence from a film.

The *Nashville* contact sheets generally have five images across and six lines down. The effect is like the individual frames in a comic book: you read across and then down to the end of the page. Contact sheets most often convey a brief period, so the images are very similar in terms of composition and content. So, for example, one contact sheet shows Mr. Green, right after the nurse has told him his wife has died, talking with Pvt. Kelly in the hospital. Mr. Green's anguish and despair are evident in the photos. The shots continue to show Mr. Green interacting with different nurses and doctors after Pvt. Kelly has left. A clear chronology is evident, with each shot just a few seconds after the previous one. Only one of these thirty shots became a Paramount publicity still, featuring Mr. Green leaning forward intently while Pvt. Kelly talks beside him. This image sums up the emotional quality of the scene perfectly and illustrates Brian Hamill's description of the still photographer's function: "to figure out what the dramatic point of each scene is and get a picture of that key moment; and to get those shots 'without disturbing anyone's concentration.'"[8] Twenty-nine images remain on the *Nashville* contact sheet, reminding us of Longworth's adage that most of the contact sheets show "aspects that someone—a star, a producer, a publicity department, a photographer, a photo editor—didn't want us to see."[9]

Although the contact sheets can be seen as existing separately from the film, they can often be a crucial means to shape our understanding of the film text. Paratexts are elements connected to the text; in the case of a film, a paratext could be a review, a DVD commentary, a podcast, or a merchandised product, all of which can influence our reception of the film text. A film still is another paratext, whether as part of a publicity campaign on initial release or, decades later, as part of an archive. Jonathan Gray describes the transformative power of paratexts: "Paratexts will regularly amplify some meanings, bury others, and they may edit or transform textual meaning in the process."[10] Gray argues that any text does not have a single, immutable meaning, but rather is affected by such contextual aspects as engaging with paratexts. Further, our own background and history also shape our interpretation of the text. Given these multiple inputs, Gray concludes that texts do not exist, they only come to be as meaning is created for each individual viewer or reader.

The Images of *Nashville*

The Altman archive contains four principal types of still images: the contact sheets; the color, posed shots by Jean Pagliuso; pictures used for wardrobe continuity; and the black-and-white Paramount publicity stills. The contact sheets include scenes, such as the one cited between Mr. Green and Pvt. Kelly, from the completed film; behind-the-scenes shots of Altman directing and interacting with the cast and his creative personnel; and scenes that feature characters and locations in the film that were either cut or never included. From the contact sheets, we discover that George Segal, costar in *California Split*, also made a guest appearance as himself, parallel to those by Julie Christie and Elliott Gould. The Pagliuso shots are dramatic, brightly colored, and apparently idealized versions of each character (e.g., a plaintive Bud Hamilton strumming a guitar, a bold Lady Pearl, with hand on hip and head raised high, peering into the distance, and a beaming Linnea singing joyfully with the gospel choir).[11] Some are obviously staged while others appear to have been captured during the shooting of a particular scene. Curiously, most are wish-fulfillment, with characters being portrayed as they would like to be seen rather than how they function in the film. Is Bud Hamilton a sensitive and stylish country singer/songwriter, as Pagliuso's image suggests, or is he an indentured servant to his famous and narcissistic father? These images build a compelling counternarrative to empower each of *Nashville*'s characters.

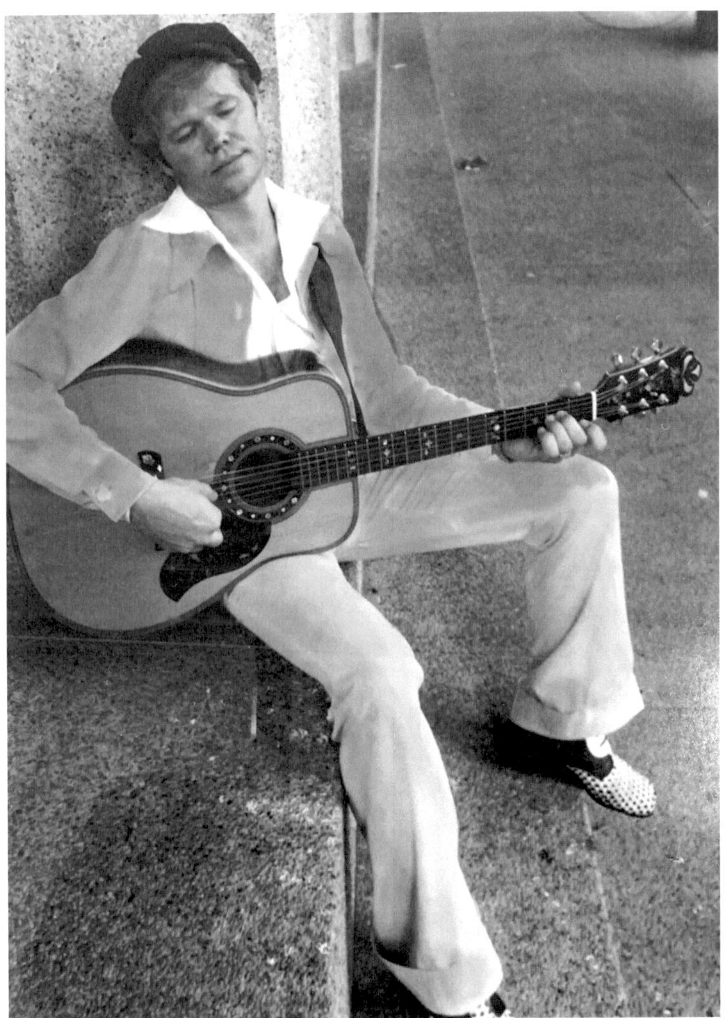

Figure 26: Glamor shot of Bud Hamilton (Dave Peel).

The wardrobe shots are simple Polaroids attached to a file listing in detail exactly what the actor was wearing in a particular scene. These shots are clearly made during production and are different from the wardrobe test shots completed prior to production to show how an actor looks in a certain costume. The wardrobe listing accounts also for changes in costuming during a scene (for example, Opal taking off her cap in a nightclub scene is noted in the file). The salient element in these shots and descriptions is the level of detail, obviously to facilitate the smooth continuity in the film's characters and settings. Additionally, the wardrobe pictures are useful for betraying a secret—showing a particular character or costume not in the completed film. In this way, the wardrobe shots shed light on deleted scenes, sometimes suggesting an unrealized potential storyline or development. We are left wondering what happened to L.A. Joan during the freeway crash or why she apparently was at the Opry Belle when Barbara Jean has her breakdown. Another hospital scene with Barbara Jean was shot, as evidenced by a different nightgown than the ones used in the existing hospital scenes. Albuquerque has a scene at the Varsity Recording Studio that is validated by contact sheets showing the character making a demo record.[12]

The Paramount black-and-white stills for *Nashville* are designed for a newspaper or magazine article or review.[13] Certain images were used often, and became iconic in representing the film: an anguished, teary-eyed Barbara Jean sitting in her hospital bed, Linnea clapping her hands while singing gospel, and Sueleen either zipping or unzipping her dress while looking in the mirror (see figure 16). All three were featured prominently as part of the *Newsweek* cover story on *Nashville*.

Other Paramount stills were used much less frequently. Interestingly, each still is accompanied by printed credits and a one- to two-sentence description of the scene. The summary can reach too far in building a potential narrative. For instance, a still of Wade talking to Albuquerque, who is hiding on the grounds of Haven Hamilton's estate, reflects a quick moment when Wade asks why Albuquerque is at the mansion. She deceives Wade, saying that she was with a date who left her. The scene ends with no resolution. Paramount's description is much more pointed: "Barbara Harris poignantly tells Robert Doqui of her burning ambition to become a leading singer in the country music entertainment world in *Nashville*, a Jerry Weintraub production of a Robert Altman film." The description fails to match the completed scene and misleads the viewer about the relationship between the two characters. In another example of the publicity building more narrative than the film contains, a shot of Mary and Tom in bed is accompanied by "Cristina Raines has a clandestine sexual liaison with Keith Carradine, whose loose, amoral lifestyle begins to inflict others with emotional scars." Again, the description gives weight and significance to the still that is not warranted given the scene within the film. The publicity efforts are devoted to giving *Nashville* a stronger narrative coherence, suggesting individual storylines to connect with the viewer rather than addressing the more daunting task of multiple storylines and characters joining together.

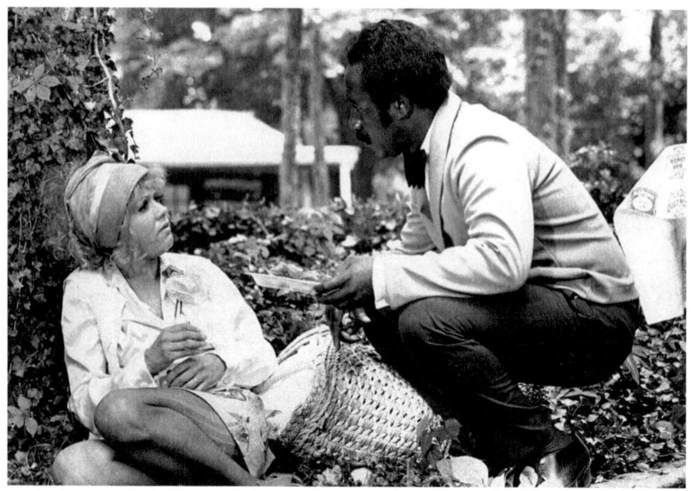

Figure 27: Wade discovers Albuquerque at Haven Hamilton's estate.

Nashville in the Contact Sheets

What can the stills tell us about Altman's design for *Nashville*? There are two primary takeaways, linked to transitions between scenes and character development, and a larger speculation based on the archival stills. These analyses demonstrate that Altman, screenwriter Tewkesbury, and their collaborators maintain great control over the developing narrative even while the many different parts may seem joined together more casually.

The contact sheets show that Altman shot several other scenes that could aid the flow between characters and their interactions, yet ultimately were omitted from the film. Consider three contact sheets: Mr. Green and Barbara Jean in her

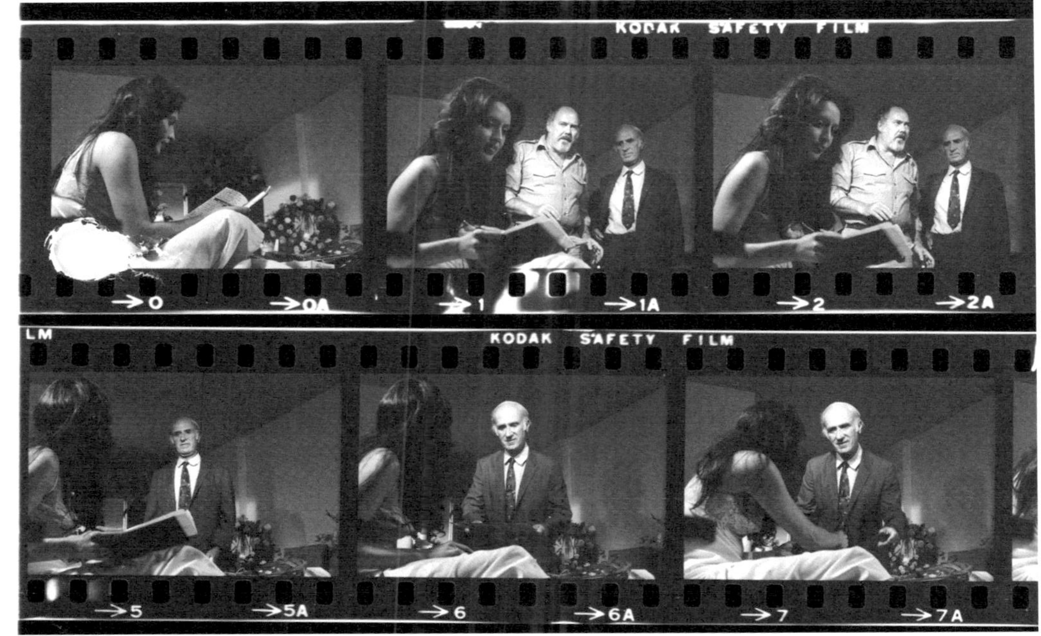

Figure 28: Mr. Green visits with Barbara Jean in her hospital room (contact sheet).

hospital room, Albuquerque and Wade at the Demon's Den nightclub, and Tom and Linnea talking after his set at the Exit/In club. The first scene shows Barbara Jean sitting up in her hospital bed chatting with Mr. Green, who cocks his head to listen more carefully to the country star. This interaction between the two characters helps to explain their connection later in the film. As Barbara Jean is leaving the hospital, she encounters Mr. Green. They have a very friendly talk in which Barbara Jean asks about Mrs. Green and she even wonders if Mrs. Green is taking her vitamin E. The dialogue is very specific in the scene and, without the evidence of the cut scene between the two, it seems unmotivated.

Albuquerque, the runaway hillbilly wife trying to become a singer, and Wade, the short-order cook marginalized by his class status and his color, are two characters on the fringes of the Nashville scene. A contact sheet reveals a lengthy dialogue between the two. The encounter happens at the back of a nightclub. Albuquerque finds a truck delivering food, and she hastily helps herself to dinner while no one is looking. Wade eventually confronts Albuquerque, who looks sheepish while continuing to enjoy the free food. As mentioned above, soon after Albuquerque is discovered sleeping in the gardens of Haven Hamilton's country home. The brief exchange between her and Wade seems curious because there is no consequence or resolution to the meeting. The missing scene on the contact sheet would certainly have given a context to the two characters interacting at Haven's home. As it is, the scene feels abbreviated, and the characters are left unconnected.

Another contact sheet captures Linnea sitting in her booth

at the back of the Exit/In club. This location centers one of the most famous *Nashville* scenes. Tom introduces his song "I'm Easy" by saying, "I'm going to dedicate this to someone kind of special who just might be here tonight." During his singing, the camera locates several women who might be the recipient of Tom's attention: Mary, Opal, L.A. Joan, and the most likely candidate, Linnea. In a masterfully shot and edited sequence, the different women, except Linnea, realize that the dedication is probably not for them. The scene finishes with the end of the song, and a little later we discover Linnea in bed with Tom at his motel room. The contact sheet shows Tom going to Linnea at the club, writing something, and passing the note to her. This moment sets up the assignation and alerts the viewer that the pair will connect, emotionally and physically.

These three scenes facilitate later action, setting in place a cause-effect relation between characters and a logic for the development of a storyline. If Altman had chosen to include the deleted scene, it would affect the viewer's interpretation of a scene later in the film. Keeping the intimate moment between Mr. Green and Barbara Jean in her hotel room might have created a softer, kinder Barbara Jean, who cares about an elderly stranger whose wife is sick. Similarly, Mr. Green could have spoken about his ailing wife, showing his connection and love for her. The simple scene would have set up the later hallway chat between the two characters and a more emotional moment when Mr. Green learns that his wife has passed. The film still functions without these scenes, but they could have bolstered a sense of continuity and a bond between the characters.

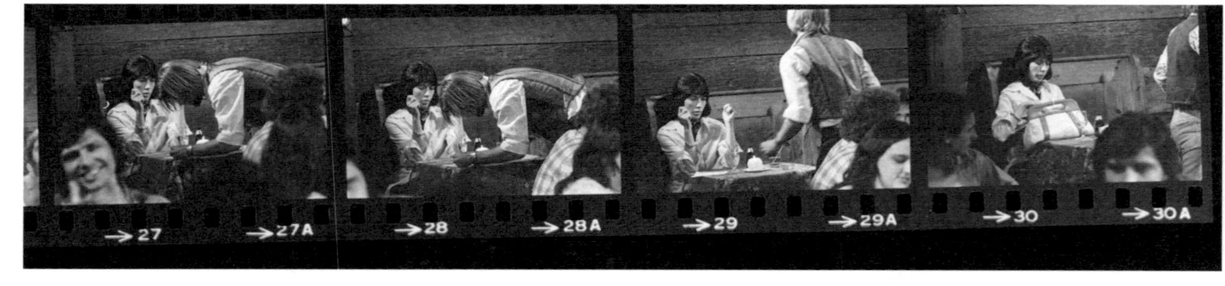

Figure 29: Tom connects with Linnea at the Exit/In club (contact sheet).

With these (and other) scenes cut, there is a greater onus on the viewer to create the missing connections and to imagine a life for the characters off-screen. Altman's approach veers from classical Hollywood storytelling, in which every element is designed to signify, and the viewer is led seamlessly through the film, not thinking about issues like continuity or causation. Admittedly, the examples cited may seem minor in the overall film, but the principle is significant.

The best example of an edit influencing viewer comprehension and storytelling is not included in the archive, but it has been documented elsewhere. Triplette gets Opal to admit that she is not really on assignment for the BBC or even a journalist. She is simply a fan/hanger-on with a crisp British accent. In an interview, Robert Altman told me that you did not need the scene because Opal's behavior made it obvious that she was a fake.[14] Geraldine Chaplin disagrees on this point. As Jan Stuart recounts, "Chaplin feels that the cut may have contributed to the intensity of distaste for her strident characterization, with the heaviest brickbats tossed by the British press. [Chaplin comments] 'Because they didn't understand that she *wasn't* from the BBC.'"[15] By deleting the revealing scene between Opal and Triplette, Altman makes the viewer consider two possibilities: that Opal's outrageous and inappropriate behavior makes her an obnoxious character or that her curious behavior betrays that Opal is not, in fact, a journalist. While Altman argues that the latter interpretation is the obvious one, many critics (and viewers) failed to grasp that Opal was a fake. Without the deleted scene, viewers can see Chaplin's performance as exaggerated; they may consider that the film to be more satirical than realistic, or question why the film is privileging the endless prattling of this character over most of the others.[16]

Other contact sheets reveal scenes that might have developed characters further. With twenty-four characters, most are present only fleetingly, even if many are on the fringes of scenes. Apart from easing transitions between scenes, these contact sheets reveal that characters could have greater depth than is evident in the final film. In most cases, the contact sheets do not contradict the character remaining in the film. Rather, they suggest greater dimensionality to a character, again offering more evidence for viewers instead of forcing them to create their own assumptions about background and motivation.

Tellingly, Opal is the subject of one contact sheet. In this case, the contact reveals a different line of action that would not be possible given footage in the completed film. I have mentioned already how Opal elicits the most negative reactions—she is truly a polarizing figure. The harshest response to Opal may be in the intimate moment when Bud Hamilton performs his song "The Heart of a Gentle Woman." Sitting at a wishing well on his father's estate, Bud plaintively sings his love song to Opal, who seems moved at first. She looks out and suddenly spots Elliott Gould. Opal abruptly leaves Bud midsong so she can cozy up to a celebrity. The scene shows Opal to be callous to the extreme, incapable of valuing a simple human connection more than an opportunity to meet a star.

The contact sheet reveals a much different story, however. Bud and Opal are together at the wishing well, and he

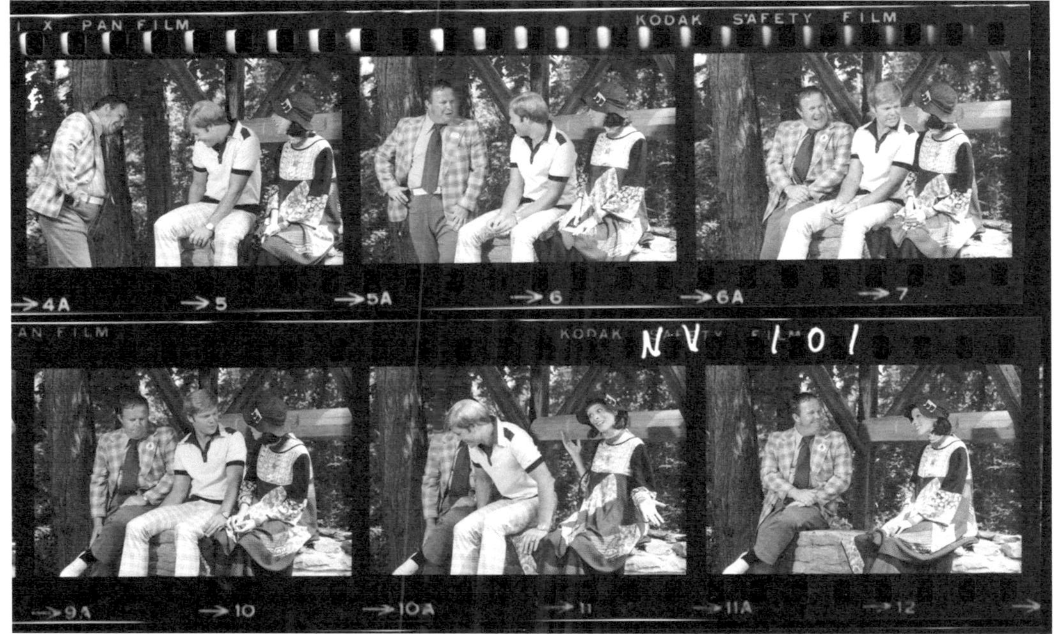

Figure 30: Opal, Bud Hamilton, and Del Reese at Haven's estate (contact sheet).

sings to her. Lawyer Del Reese (Ned Beatty) sits down next to the pair. Bud eventually leaves Opal and Del together. They spend some time chatting and eventually both depart the wishing well. What could be happening? Bud might be called away to help his father while Del is left to escort Opal during her visit to the Haven Hamilton estate. If Altman had opted for this turn of events, Opal would have been perhaps somewhat more relatable, forming a bond with Bud rather than dumping him cruelly. Altman's choice yields a sharper-edged Opal, desperate for celebrity, while the contact sheet potentially humanizes her.

A contact sheet can display a scene Altman deleted for strategic reasons. Albuquerque is played by established actress and singer Barbara Harris, who had appeared in the Broadway musicals *The Apple Tree* and *On a Clear Day You Can See Forever.* Altman wanted Albuquerque's rendition of "It Don't Worry Me" to be surprising to the audience, who would suddenly discover that the runaway wife was a gifted singer. Accordingly, Altman trimmed several scenes of Albuquerque singing earlier in the film, such as her performance singing at the speedway. The contact sheet in the Altman archives shows Albuquerque in a recording studio cutting her demo record and accompanied by Frog (Richard Baskin) on guitar.[17] Albuquerque starts in the recording booth, but then joins Frog in the musician's area to talk. As with other examples, Altman's trims can limit the definition of a character. As is, Albuquerque plays a small and often silent role in the film until the finale.

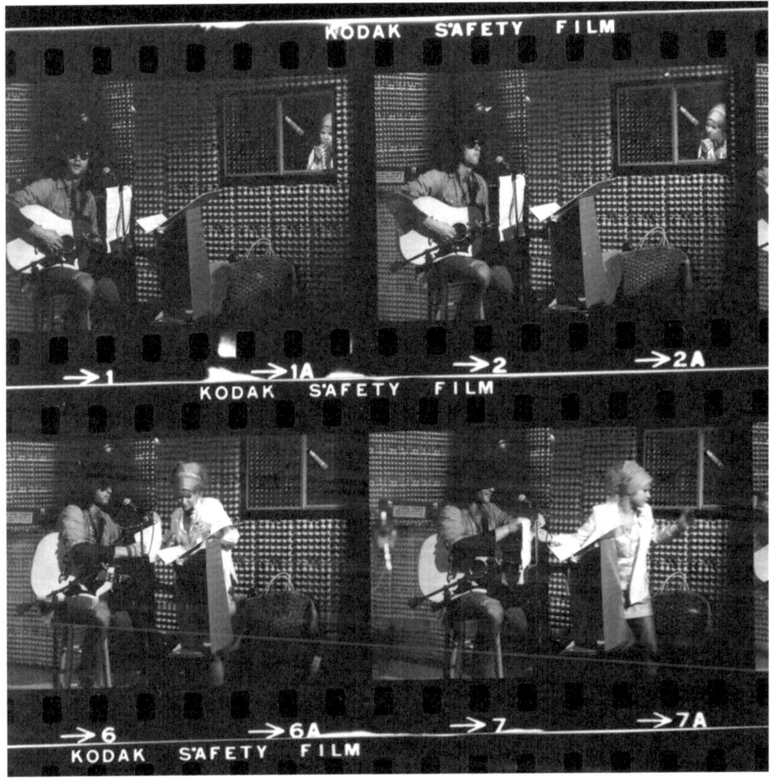

Figure 31: Albuquerque in the recording studio (contact sheet).

The Contradictions of Pvt. Kelly

The contact sheets revealed added dimensions to a character or facilitated transitions between scenes in a smooth manner. Of course, I am framing these deleted scenes based on the character that is present in the film. The "surviving" footage takes precedence in forming an assessment of the character. Most of the contact sheets offer minor adjustments to the character presentations in the completed film. Yet one set of images substantially complicates a character, perhaps reversing an interpretation gathered from the film.

Pvt. Kelly (Scott Glenn), like many *Nashville* characters, hovers on the edge of the action without expressing much. In the final third, Pvt. Kelly, in a sudden burst, tells Mr. Green that he is on leave to see Barbara Jean, whom his mother saved after the singer's fire baton accident. In the finale, Pvt. Kelly wrestles the gun from Kenny, although Kelly is unable to save Barbara Jean from the assassin. The ending frames Kelly as a hero, stopping Kenny from shooting further.

Two contact sheets, though, make Pvt. Kelly's story more intricate. The first shows Pvt. Kelly, late at night in the hospital, evading a security guard who is deep in conversation with a nurse. Kelly walks down the hospital corridor and pauses before entering Barbara Jean's room. Kelly peers into the door jam intensely, frozen before he makes his way into the room. In the film, the scene shows his walk through the corridor and cuts to him entering the room. The pause (captured by over fifteen shots on the contact sheet) is entirely missing. Adding this moment of hesitation fosters the idea that Kelly knows that he should not be entering the room. His intent at this point is unknown. Does he mean harm for Barbara Jean? Consider two pieces of additional data. In an encounter earlier that day, Tom sidled up to Kelly, saying, "Hiya sergeant—kill anyone this week?" This is a snide, mean comment certainly, but it also joins the idea of violence to Kelly. Another piece of evidence is from the published *Nashville* screenplay; note that the action of writing the note is not depicted in the final film:

> *INTERIOR. BARBARA-JEAN'S ROOM.*
> *Pvt. Kelly enters the darkened room which now looks like a funeral parlor. Barbara-Jean looks like Sleeping Beauty. He puts the flowers in her water pitcher, then sits down beside the bed and writes the following note: "When I die and go to heaven / I want you to come along / and be an angel with me."*[18]

The screenplay entry could be read as Pvt. Kelly being either a protector or someone who wants to control Barbara Jean. Both readings are defensible, given Kelly's words matched with his unlawful entry into Barbara Jean's hospital room. Added to the furtive looks before entering her room and Tom's casual comment, Pvt. Kelly takes on a more malicious quality while the film's depiction is more favorable, offering a character who is likable and without ill intent.

As a character, Pvt. Kelly becomes even more of a puzzle in a second contact sheet. In this scene, missing from the film, Kelly confronts a man at the Opry Belle where Barbara Jean has just performed. At first, the two talk, but Kelly shoves the

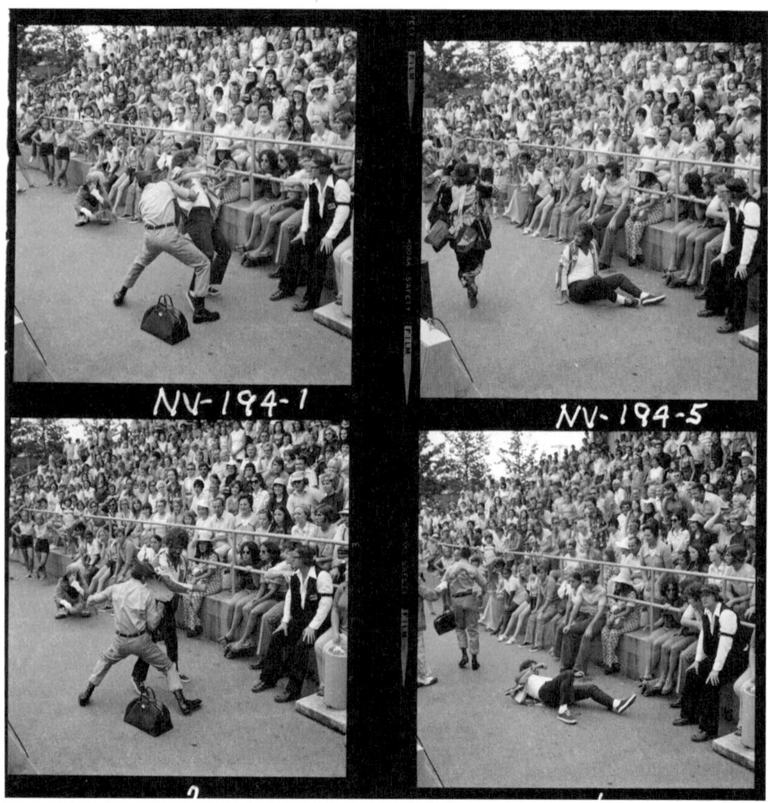

Figure 32: Pvt. Kelly in a violent confrontation at the Opry Belle (contact sheet).

person and proceeds to knock him down violently. Doubled over in pain, Kelly's adversary cannot even respond to the attack. He is left crumpled on the walkway near the stage. The crowds in the stands look on as the fight continues but no one intervenes.

Combined with the other evidence, the Opry Belle contact sheet creates a different image for the character. The possibility of violence is reinforced. We do not know how this aggression might be displayed. The attack scene, for instance, could be the result of Kelly protecting or defending Barbara Jean after she stopped performing so abruptly.[19] It could also be the result of a combat soldier struggling with posttraumatic stress disorder, who has a tendency to use violence to solve problems. The attack could color some of the previous encounters with Kelly, making them seem more sinister rather neutral or positive.

Playing Billiards in the Archives

By entertaining such a contrary view of the character, I am indulging in speculative consumption. Jonathan Gray explains that our engagement with paratexts leads viewers to create "certain meanings and interpretations" of the film. Gray cites elements such as the poster, the marketing campaign, the source materials, and a host of other paratexts.[20] My activity of combing through the *Nashville* images, stills, marketing, and other ephemera does not inform an initial viewing of the film. Rather, I am confounding with additional data my own interpretations of a film seen many times, considering other directions for the characters, and seeking to augment or refine my accepted vision of *Nashville*'s characters and world.

Filmmaker Rebecca Baron, whose film work is often comprised of still photography and found footage, describes her research for a project in these terms: "For me, the process is associative. I think of it as a billiard game with the ideas banking off the sidewalls, leading to unexpected trajectories."[21] Similarly, my exploration of the *Nashville* stills was based on discovering images not in the film and then attempting to reconcile them with my knowledge of *Nashville*'s narrative. This exercise reveals that, had they been used, the deleted scenes would have facilitated a smoother transition between scenes and enhanced our understanding of character, and at times relationships between characters. The contact sheets mostly reveal elements that fit with the character on film. These images usually present additional facets of the character that paint the person in more depth. The curious example of the Pvt. Kelly contact sheets, however, complicates our understanding of the character.

The Enigmatic Image

A single image can expand the world of the film and offer clues on how the film was constructed. To close, consider a color image from the archives of Barbara Jean singing at the Opry Belle. She is on stage, and the large crowd is attentive and interested in her performance. At first, this image seems ordinary: a good shot of Ronee Blakley singing as Barbara Jean, nothing more. Yet two small differences from the film are tell-

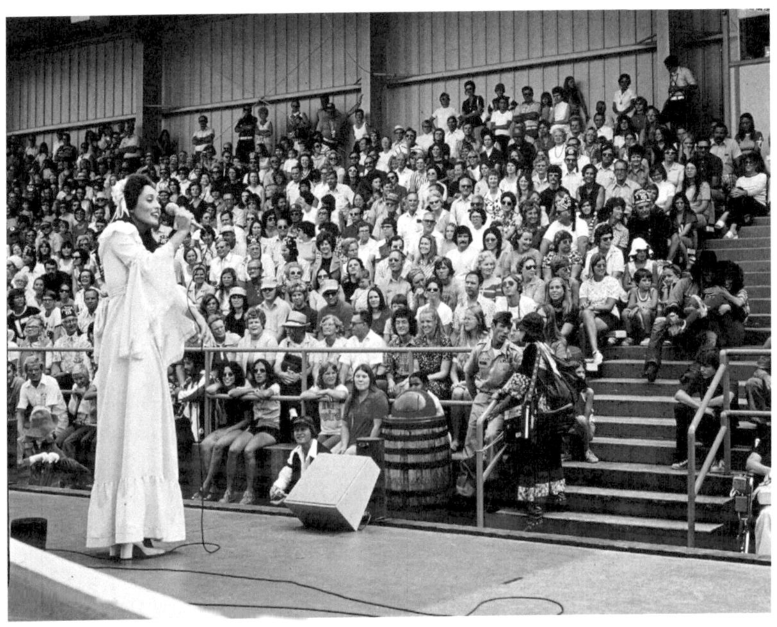

Figure 33: Barbara Jean's Opry Belle concert with Frog and L.A Joan in the aisle and no Kenny (contact sheet).

ing. On the far right, we discover Frog and L.A. Joan laughing and cuddling. In the film, these characters do not appear in this scene. Their presence in the still reminds us that Altman has an expansive view of his story world: characters inhabit scenes even if they do not appear on camera. In this way, the world of *Nashville*, the film, becomes larger, as viewers realize that other characters exist just beyond the cinematic frame.

The other insight from the image is an absence: Kenny is

not seated next to Pvt. Kelly, who talks with Opal during the concert. In the film, Kenny looks over furtively as Pvt. Kelly describes his experience in Vietnam. The image shows that Kenny was added at some point to the scene, perhaps as a contrast to Pvt. Kelly, Barbara Jean's self-appointed savior. We can conclude that Altman wanted to make the connection between Kenny and Kelly in this scene. The director sets the characters side by side so viewers can compare the two. One will be Barbara Jean's assassin and the other her hero. Even though Kenny is silent in the Opry Belle scene, his presence indicates that Altman sees a bond between the characters. The image confirms this by showing how the film was altered to add Kenny to the scene. Altman's *Nashville* is sprawling and alive yet very designed and deliberate at the same time. The still images give us ample evidence of this opposition.

Coda
After the Archives

These takes on *Nashville* have centered on three areas: aesthetic, social, and commercial. Aesthetically, Altman's technique is evident through analyzing the contact sheets (i.e., the deletions highlight elements of Altman's stylistic choices) and through isolating Tewkesbury's contribution to the film (i.e., leaving Altman's additions in content and style as the focus). In the social realm, I highlight how characters and their actions and interactions shape representations that both reflect and reinforce divisions within mainstream society. Commercially, I mainly look at the advertising, showing how *Nashville* was framed through critical acclaim, yet the muddled attempts by Paramount to position the film in the marketplace led to public confusion and apathy, fostering the notion that for viewers *Nashville* was more challenging than entertaining. Altman's thwarted attempts to maximize the popularity of the film demonstrate that he was interested in his commercial viability, which is rarely thought of as a concern for the director. Considering these analyses together, one can see how creativity, commercial impulses, and exploitation are tied together in *Nashville*'s history, and, I would posit, in American studio filmmaking, then and now.

Although I'm returning to a film I have been close to for more than half a century, my archival exploration has made me look at *Nashville* in a different light. As with any artwork, the perspective of the viewer is molded by their own place, time, and background. The archival artifacts are new data that can be employed to revisit *Nashville* and consider, both textually and contextually, how it functions after all these decades. This exercise has illuminated analytical, creative, and textual dimensions and modified my understanding of the film and its power.

Tracing Pathways

My investigations in the archive rarely led to a lightbulb moment such as finding a document that would shed new light on the creative process of filmmaking. More often, my process would involve looking for disjunctures or fissures between different elements in the archive. Screenplay drafts, images, and memos created a tapestry of creative inputs. Interviews with key collaborators offered another thread of information about the creative process, albeit one that was sometimes dulled by the space of fifty years. Rather than explain how the film came to fruition, I discovered what the film might have been, an alternative direction that could have been taken.

The contact sheets offer a clear example of this option, sometimes detailing excised scenes that would have changed the trajectory of the narrative or the audience's conception of a character. The sheets offer second-by-second records of another *Nashville*, complicating certain characters and diminishing others. Earlier drafts of the script amplify some of these differences. Joan Tewkesbury's detailed character descriptions and isolated incidents and exchanges betray a different tone than we see in the finished film. Another *Nashville* might have provided more searing political and social commentary, largely without moments of levity or redemption.

Through piecing together these forgotten directions, one can see both Tewkesbury's huge contribution to the design of the film and the tonal differences introduced by Altman. The archival materials give greater shape and dimension to the characters. They also evidence how Altman's approach to paring back description and background allows the audience to have more control in creating their own narrative for the film. Altman's tendency is to embrace realism and freedom, whereas Tewkesbury is more concerned with character psychology and narrative development. This dynamic tension between the opposing forces gives *Nashville* vitality.

To give a concrete example of this dynamic, consider that Tewkesbury's earlier screenplay draft ended with Triplette punching Hal Phillip Walker after Walker made a wisecrack immediately following Barbara Jean's assassination. While this may be emotionally satisfying, Altman's ending—scanning through the crowd as they all sing "It Don't Worry Me," led by Albuquerque—is more ambiguous. It leaves the viewer to consider how an act of violence can be forgotten and integrated into American culture in a heartbeat.

Money Matters

Altman's desire to make *Nashville* a film with strong commercial appeal is another theme throughout the archival exploration. The New Hollywood era, pre-*Jaws* and pre–*Star Wars* (1977), is usually marked by freedom of expression unconstrained by commercial considerations. Many of the changes from Tewkesbury's script add to the film moments of lightness, fun, and even farce. Recall that the leading critical quote on the dancing microphone poster appeared to position the film as a comedy ("'the funniest epic vision of America to ever reach the screen'—*New Yorker* magazine"). Altman's ability to capitalize on the actors' contributions to the film's humor are noteworthy, too. Geraldine Chaplin's offbeat soliloquies add to the film and shift it tonally, and Karen Black's ability to telegraph her vain character visually and through throwaway lines similarly helps to give the film a light touch.

Altman maximized his publicity for the film in the hope of attracting a mass audience. As has been noted, the talking point that the actors wrote their own songs is rather overstated (some were repurposed; others were a collaboration with Richard Baskin). Through this project, I discovered that Altman's preferred poster would have been based on the William Myers cartoon artwork, which was much more inviting and evocative than either the singing microphone or the jean-jacket ad.

These signals point to Altman's realization that being an auteur would only be valuable to a point—eventually he would need another box office hit on the level of *M*A*S*H*. Altman's interest in marketing and publicity for *Nashville* highlights the stakes of the film after so many relative financial failures in a row. Is it possible that Altman's efforts to add lightness to the film were motivated to make it more appealing to a general audience? Again, this proposition goes against the grain of the New Hollywood auteur, but it may speak to the commercial realities of working with the mainstream studios and distributors of the time.

Entertainment and Politics

Nashville's most notable achievement may be its snapshot of the American political landscape. At the time of its release, critics frequently mentioned the parallels between politics and entertainment, including the trajectory for success and fame in both arenas. The possibility of a third-party political candidate was discussed as well. After more than fifty years, the intersection of entertainment and politics we see in *Nashville* has proven to be the defining factor in our media landscape. In the movie, candidate Hal Phillip Walker is represented endlessly with logos, campaign outfits, stickers, and blaring (but ignored) messages from the traveling van. Especially for the mid-1970s, the campaign relies heavily on image and style, with, tellingly, no glimpses of the candidate himself. We are left with the dealmaker (Triplette in this case), the deals, and the selling of the politician. Dealmaking and salesmanship have buoyed American political discourse of the last half century. How far are Walker's "New Roots for the Nation" from Ronald Reagan's legendary "It's Morning in America Again"

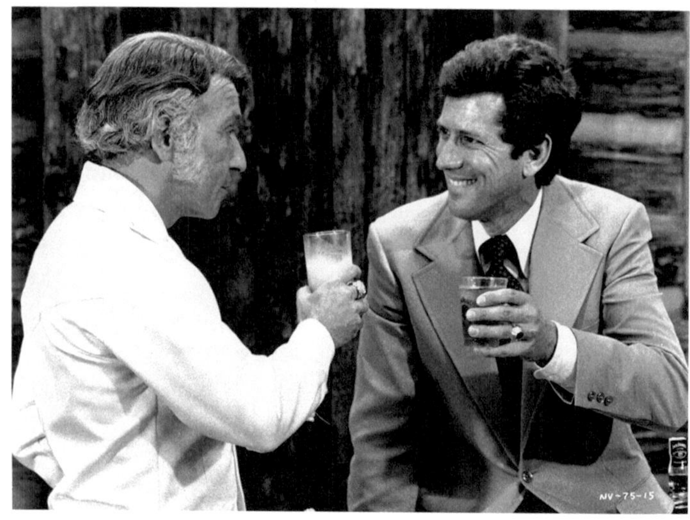

Figure 34: Triplette, the dealmaker (right).

campaign in 1984? Pushing heavily for traditional values, hard work, small-town life, and nostalgia, Reagan, guided by advertising executive Hal Riney, distilled an emotional appeal that has shaped much of political advertising since that time. Interestingly, apart from the final tag, Reagan is missing from his own ad. Everyday people, homespun wisdom, and shots of the American flag reign supreme.

Certainly, image management over the decades has crafted presidents on both sides of aisle, from Barack Obama's effortless, understated cool to George W. Bush's down-home Texan charm. If *Nashville* illuminated the importance of image over ideology and entertainment over politics, the logical endpoint is the forty-fifth and forty-seventh president, Donald

J. Trump. With years of media training hosting *The Apprentice* and his ability to utter pithy catchphrases with conviction ("You're fired!"), Trump dominance shows us that image has become all in American life, with ideology and message all just noise, like the ignored Walker campaign messages. In the digital era our political appetite is for entertainment: the entertainment of a well-defined image suggesting wealth, power, and control. We no longer need the middleman of the country-and-western stars in the rally; the candidate is entertainment himself, generating strong emotions from all sides, as evidenced by Donald Trump on his 2024 campaign stage simply moving to the music of his favorite songs rather than making speeches. America buys into a persona and an image, rather than focusing on issues and social concerns.

Over time, the America portrayed in *Nashville* just seems to be emphasized rather than modified or progressed. Was Altman a prognosticator, or was he merely lucky in forecasting that America is stuck in an endless loop? Haven Hamilton, grazed by a bullet and bleeding, pleads for "somebody to sing," handing the mic to the dazed but talented Albuquerque. Skip forward half a century, Donald J. Trump, grazed by a bullet and bleeding, raises one fist in defiance at his campaign rally in Pennsylvania. In both cases, we "keep-a-goin'" because that's the American credo. Altman's film, and the artifacts from his archive, illuminate how a work of art can be meaningful across generations. *Nashville* reminds us that art can be a mirror and a way to transform ourselves as well.

> "That wasn't an ending. It was just a stopping point."
>
> **—Robert Altman**

Notes

Preface

1. "Under the Influence: Steve James on *Nashville*," Criterioncollection.com; https://www.youtube.com/watch?v=h0lBD6cLtFk&t=13s

2. The British Columbia Film Classification office at that time assigned ratings of General, Mature, or Restricted to each film, with content warnings (e.g., some swearing, occasional scenes of violence, nudity throughout, etc.).

3. Les Wedman, "The Road to Nashville," *Vancouver Sun*, July 18, 1975, 4–5.

4. Charles Michener, "Altman's Opryland Epic," *Newsweek*, June 30, 1975, 46.

5. I interviewed Maysie Hoy for a research project on *3 Women* and was able to thank her for this kindness, only forty-seven years after the act had taken place.

6. The interviews for this article included Scott Glenn, Michael Murphy, Keith Carradine, Lily Tomlin, Karen Black, Henry Gibson, Barbara Harris, Joan Tewkesbury, and Robert Altman.

7. Kurt Vonnegut Jr., "*Nashville*: A Shadow Play of What We Have Become and Where We Might Look for Wisdom," *Vogue*, June 1975, 91.

Chapter 1

1. David A. Cook, *Lost Illusions: American Cinema in the Shadow of Watergate and Vietnam 1970–1979* (University of California Press, 2000), 9.

2. My book *High Concept: Movies and Marketing in Hollywood* (University of Texas Press, 1994) considers the transition from the New Hollywood period to high-concept filmmaking defined by marketing-friendly premises, simple narratives, and an often distinctive visual style.

3. Connie Byrne and William O. Lopez, "*Nashville*," *Film Quarterly* 20.2 (Winter 1975–1976), 18.

4. Charles Schreger, "Altman, Dolby, and the Second Sound Revolution." *Film Sound: Theory and Practice*, ed. Elisabeth Weis and John Belton (Columbia University Press, 1985), 350.

5. Jay Beck, "The Democratic Voice: Altman's Sound Aesthetics in the 1970s," *A Companion to Robert Altman*, ed. Adrian Danks (Wiley Blackwell, 2015), 185.

6. Quoted in Mitchell Zuckoff, *Robert Altman: The Oral Biography* (Alfred A. Knopf, 2009), 289.

Chapter 2

1. Maya Montañez Smukler, *Liberating Hollywood: Women Directors and the Feminist Reform of 1970s American Cinema* (Rutgers University Press, 2019).

2. Mentioned in Terry Curtis Fox, "'*Nashville* Chats': An Interview with Robert Altman," *Chicago Reader*, July 4, 1975, 10; *Nashville* scrapbooks, University of Michigan Special Collections Robert Altman Archive.

3. Zuckoff, 274.

4. Jim Ridley, "Look Back in Anger," *Nashville Scene*, November 9, 1995, 28.

5. Nick Dawson, Joan Tewkesbury interview, *Filmmaker* magazine, December 2013.

6. Production designer Polly Platt strongly disagreed with Altman's decision to end with an assassination, and quit working on the film after this point.

7. Stuart, 60.

8. Meredith Danluck, interview with Joan Tewkesbury, *Interview*, October 22, 2015: https://www.interviewmagazine.com/film/joan-tewkesbury

9. Certainly, Opal and Lady Pearl have a much lower profile in Tewkesbury's screenplay. Their visibility in the completed film derives largely from these lauded scenes (and no doubt from their performance within the film as a whole).

10. Interview with Joan Tewkesbury, Craft/Visual History, Director's Guild of America, December 5, 2006; https://www.dga.org/Craft/VisualHistory/Interviews/Joan-Tewkesbury

11. Frank Segers, "Robert Altman on the Verge of Shaking 'Bad Boy' Reputation," *Variety*, June 11, 1975 (University of Michigan Special Collections Robert Altman Archive).

12. Altman, Kathryn Reed, and Giulia D'Agnolo Vallan. *Altman* (Abrams, 2014), 118.

13. Alex Lewin, "It Happened in Nashville," *Premiere*, July 2000, 93.

14. Lewin, 93.

15. Sally Quinn, "You Either Love or Hate Altman," *Los Angeles Times*, July 6, 1975, 30.

16. "Ronee Blakley: Out of the Guitars and Gritty Truth about *Nashville* Comes a Star," *People*, July 7, 1975 (University of Michigan Special Collections Robert Altman Archive).

17. Grace Glueck, "Nashville Team Credits Coach," *New York Times*, June 20, 1975 (University of Michigan Special Collections Robert Altman Archive).

18. Harry Kloman, Lloyd Michaels, and Virginia Wright Wexman, "Interview with Robert Altman," *Robert Altman Interviews*, ed. David Sterritt (University Press of Mississippi, 2000), 114.

19. Quoted in Peter Biskind, *Easy Riders, Raging Bulls: How the Sex-Drugs-and-Rock'n'roll Generation Saved Hollywood* (Simon & Schuster, 1998), 97–98.

20. Author's interview with Joan Tewkesbury, April 25, 2024.

21. Nick Dawson, "'That's the Movie, That's the Kind of Overlapping Mess That Bob Loves': Joan Tewkesbury on Writing *Nashville*"; https://filmmakermagazine.com/82780-thats-the-movie-thats-the-kind-of-overlapping-mess-that-bob-loves-joan-tewkesbury-on-writing-nashville/

22. Terry Curtis Fox, "*Nashville* Chats: Interview with Robert Altman," *Chicago Reader*, July 4, 1975, 10 (University of Michigan Special Collections Robert Altman Archive).

23. Dawson, "'That's the Movie," https://filmmakermagazine.com/82780-thats-the-movie-thats-the-kind-of-overlapping-mess-that-bob-loves-joan-tewkesbury-on-writing-nashville/

24. Author's interview with Joan Tewkesbury, April 25, 2024.

25. This book should be contrasted with the *Brewster McCloud* paperback, which includes a behind-the-scenes shooting diary, the finished shooting script (with no attribution), and the original screenplay, *Brewster McCloud's Flying Machine*, by Doran William Cannon. This composition at least gives credit to the original screenwriter (and acknowledges that the final film is markedly different than this screenplay).

26. Quinn, "You Either Love or Hate Altman," 30.

27. Tewkesbury connected with Bill and Taffy Danoff, who had been part of a trio, Fat Chance, with John Denver as the third member of the group. The Danoffs accompanied Tewkesbury on her first trip to Nashville.

The Bill, Mary, and Tom trio was loosely inspired by this real-life trio. Altman even considered Taffy Danoff to play Mary in his film.

28. Steven Paul, "50 Years Ago: Opry Legend Stringbean Akeman Is Murdered," savingcountrymusic.com, https://www.savingcountrymusic.com/50-years-ago-opry-legend-stringbean-akeman-is-murdered/

29. "Dialogue on Film: Joan Tewkesbury," *American Film* (March 1979), 43.

30. The moment in which Haven Hamilton offers Tommy Brown some watermelon and is scolded by Pearl for being insensitive is a gag connected to race in the finished film.

31. F. Anthony Macklin, "The Artist and the Multitude Are Natural Enemies," in *Robert Altman Interviews*, 72.

32. Author's interview with Joan Tewkesbury, April 25, 2024.

33. Author's interview with Joan Tewkesbury, April 25, 2024.

34. Connie Bryne and William O. Lopez, "Nashville," *Film Quarterly* 20.2 (Winter 1975–1976), 21.

35. The background on the game's development in conjunction with the film can be seen in many documents in the Altman archives at the University of Michigan. Altman and his team sought copyright protection for the name, design, and concept of the game.

36. Author's interview with Alan Rudolph, October 23, 2023.

37. Patrick McGilligan, *Robert Altman: Jumping Off the Cliff* (St. Martin's Press, 1989), 414.

38. Author's interview with Joan Tewkesbury, April 25, 2024.

Chapter 3

1. Altman was scheduled to make a film of E. L. Doctorow's epic about America at the turn of the twentieth century, *Ragtime*. Sadly, producer Dino De Laurentiis removed Altman from the project, given the lackluster box office of *Buffalo Bill and the Indians*. Milos Forman eventually made *Ragtime* for producer De Laurentiis in 1981.

2. Helene Keyssar, *Robert Altman's America* (Oxford University Press, 1991).

3. Naming the candidate Hal Phillip Walker, the political strategist Thomas Hal Phillips clearly offers a funny gloss on his own name.

4. J. Hoberman, "NASHVILLE Contra JAWS, or 'The Imagination of Disaster Revisited,'" *The Last Great American Picture Show: New Hollywood Cinema in the 1970s*, ed. Thomas Elsaesser, Noel King, Alexander Howarth (Amsterdam University Press, 2004), 200.

5. Ken Dancyger, *Storytelling for Film and Television: From First Word to Last Frame* (Routledge, 2019), 144.

6. Steven Abrahams, "Buying Nashville," *Jump Cut* 9 (1975), 6–7; and J. Hoberman, 210.

7. Joan Tewkesbury explains how Geraldine Chaplin wanted to interject about the Bay of Pigs during Pearl's Kennedy speech. This anecdote would have added a new dimension to the simple Kennedy adulation.

8. Mitchell Zuckoff, *Robert Altman: The Oral Biography* (Knopf), 88.

9. Aaron Latham, "Jimmy Carter's Clockwork Campaign Style," *New York*, May 17, 1976, 37.

10. For a useful analysis of the connection between Carter and Hal Phillip Walker, consult J. Hoberman, "Rerunning for President: Altman in Astoria," *Village Voice*, July 14, 1992, 57.

11. Quoted in Michael Louis Levine, PhD dissertation, "A Heightened Sense of Messiness: JR, Nashville, The Dead Father and the Refusal of Narrative," Rice University, 1996, 86.

12. David Sterritt, "Robert Altman: Documentaries, Dreamscapes, and Dialogic Cinema," *When Movies Mattered: The New Hollywood Revisited*, ed. Jon Lewis and Jonathan Kirschner (Cornell University Press, 2019), 78–79.

13. Peter Lev, *American Film of the 70s: Conflicting Visions* (University of Texas Press, 2000), 63.

14. While Triplette is one step away from being a politician, Altman uses Michael Murphy, who plays Triplette, as a political candidate in *Tanner 88* and *Tanner on Tanner*. Tellingly, his manner and style of delivery are very similar as both Triplette and Tanner.

15. Lev, 63.

16. Tom Wicker, "A Cascade of Greed, Cruelty, Hysteria," *New York Times*, June 15, 1975, Part 2: 1.

17. Kathryn Cramer Brownell, "Gerald Ford, *Saturday Night Live*, and the Development of the Entertainer in Chief," *Presidential Studies Quarterly* 46.4 (December 2016), 925.

18. Hal Erickson, *From Beautiful Downtown Burbank: A Critical History of Rowan and Martin's Laugh-In, 1968–1973* (McFarland, 2009), 168.

19. Brownell, 939.

20. Christos Tsiolakis, "Altman: The Artist in Middle Age," *A Companion to Robert Altman*, ed. Adrian Danks (Wiley-Blackwell, 2015), 392.

21. For a useful examination of trans representation in that film, see Sarah Sinwell's essay in *Refocus: The Later Films and Legacy of Robert Altman*, ed. Lisa Dombrowski and Justin Wyatt (Edinburgh University Press, 2021), 159–71.

22. The outliers are Star (Albuquerque's husband), the Tricycle Man, and the blank assassin Kenny. Both Star and the Tricycle Man are peripheral to the action with hardly any dialogue. Kenny, by design, is left mysterious so his role in the finale can be a surprise.

23. Keyssar, 159.

24. Sterritt, 79.

25. The remaining female characters are Mary, who is dependent both professionally and personally on her relationships with her two male partners, and Lady Pearl, who is somewhat inscrutable, with Altman painting her sometimes as a loudmouth and at other times as a reflective and tired melancholic.

26. As mentioned earlier, Wade's confrontation of Tommy Brown as a sellout also fits into this pattern of defining Tommy solely by race.

27. Jan Stuart, *The Nashville Chronicles: The Making of Robert Altman's Masterpiece* (Simon & Schuster, 2000), 190.

28. Robert Niemi, *The Cinema of Robert Altman: Hollywood Maverick* (Wallflower Press, 2016), 77.

29. Richard Ness, "'Doing Some Replacin'': Gender, Genre, and the Subversion of Dominant Ideology in the Music Scene," *Robert Altman: Critical Essays*, ed. Rick Armstrong (McFarland, 2011), 50.

30. Letters from Henry Gibson, both dated September 3, 1976 (one to Mr. Petrich; one "To Whom It May Concern"). The letters are in the *Nashville* folder of the Robert Altman Archive, University of Michigan Special Collections.

31. Stuart, 196.

32. Gibson letter dated September 3, 1976, "To Whom It May Concern," Robert Altman Archive, University of Michigan Special Collections.

33. Stuart, 35–36.

34. Gayle Sherwood Magee, *Robert Altman's Soundtracks: Film, Music and Sound from M*A*S*H to A Prairie Home Companion* (Oxford University Press, 2014), 125.

35. Magee, 128.

36. Magee, 121.

37. Letter from Paul S. Almond, ABC Records, to Warner Bros. Records, October 10, 1975; Robert Altman Archive, University of Michigan Special Collections.

38. Jan Stuart explains how this disagreement between Blakley and ABC Records / Landscape damaged her relationship with Altman. Blakley claims that she lost a role in Alan Rudolph's *Welcome to L.A.* because of the fallout.

39. Letter from Harry Birdwell to Paramount Pictures, October 1, 1975; Robert Altman Archive, University of Michigan Special Collections.

40. Letter from Mitchell, Silberberg, & Knupp to Elaine Bradish, Landscape Films, October 29, 1975; Robert Altman Archive, University of Michigan Special Collections.

41. Letter from Elaine Bradish to Harry Birdwell, December 11, 1975; Robert Altman Archive, University of Michigan Special Collections.

42. Robert Self, *Robert Altman's Subliminal Reality* (University of Minnesota Press, 2002).

43. Other Paramount films from the era (including *Chinatown* [1974], *The Parallax View* [1974], and *The Day of the Locust* [1975]), also offer a critique of the American dream. Paramount's shift to more thoughtful films such as *Nashville* and *The Day of the Locust* links to Richard Sylbert taking over from Robert Evans as production chief for the studio. A former production designer, Sylbert was unafraid to gamble on these serious films, along with Bernardo Bertolucci's *1900* (1976). Sylbert's commitment was rewarded financially with his decision to develop *Looking for Mr. Goodbar* (1977) for the studio.

Chapter 4

1. "Self-Indulgence to B.O. Click, Trend for 'Difficult' Altman," *Variety*, June 11, 1975, 4.

2. "Lengthy 'Nashville,' 55G in Pair," *Variety*, June 18, 1975, 8.

3. *Variety*, June18, July 9, and July 23, 1975.

4. Justin Wyatt, "Economic Constraints/Economic Opportunities: Robert Altman as Auteur," *The Velvet Light Trap* 38 (Fall 1996), 56.

5. Box Office Mojo reports a worldwide box office gross of $81.6 million for the film.

6. Timothy Corrigan, *A Cinema Without Walls: Movies and Culture after Vietnam* (Rutgers University Press, 1991), 107.

7. The actual gross, according to *Variety* (March 3, 1971), was $969,130.

8. The Jack Davis poster was used after an initial release with a more elegant Richard Amsel image of Marlowe (Elliott Gould) with his cat was discarded. Both Altman and United Artists executive David Picker take credit for the revised campaign. Set as a vivid cartoon image recalling the *Mad Magazine* film recaps, Davis's first word bubble is given to Altman: "Hi! I'm high-powered director Robert Altman, and I'm here on location filming my latest high-powered movie *The Long Goodbye*." Sadly, the new approach also failed to entice audiences during the initial release.

9. Hal Erickson, *"From Beautiful Downtown Burbank": A Critical History of* Rowan and Martin's Laugh-In, *1968–1973* (McFarland and Company, 2000), 258.

10. In 1976, Black appeared in Alfred Hitchcock's final film, *Family Plot*. Although a high-profile film, it also failed to give the actress a platform for a more sustained leading-actor career. Black continued acting through the decades, albeit in smaller, independent films.

11. Jerry Weintraub and Rich Cohen, *When I Stop Talking, You'll Know I'm Dead* (Twelve Hachette Book Group, 2010), 166.

12. David Marc, *Demographic Vistas: Television in American Culture* (University of Pennsylvania Press, 1996): 62.

13. Erickson, 184.

14. Erickson, 185.

15. The Paramount archives house another unused advertising image for *Nashville*: a corn husk set onto a record player. Each kernel of corn has a picture of a *Nashville* actor on it. The corn theme suggests *Hee Haw*'s cornfield location, although the connection between the corn and the record is not immediately apparent from the image.

16. The jean-jacket ad was used widely in the film's release, including in newspaper ads in Albuquerque, Birmingham, Boise, Boston, Calgary, Ft. Worth, Kansas City, Miami, Minneapolis, Montreal, Ottawa, Philadelphia, Phoenix, Sacramento, San Francisco, Saskatoon, and Vancouver. Markets such as Boston and San Francisco opened with the microphone ad but this was transitioned to the jean-jacket ad over time. The film's opening in Nashville at the Martin Theater on August 8, 1975, two months after the New York release, also featured the jean jacket with the additional text "*Nashville* Comes Home."

17. As the weeks progressed, the film's newspaper ads eventually shrank to the just the tagline "One. Two. Three. Go See . . ." and the license plate.

18. Dan Perri, *Hollywood Titles Designer: A Life in Film* (Finchley Central Films, 2020), 11.

19. Joseph Gelmis, "Altman Beating Bushes to Sell *Nashville* to the Masses," *Denver Post*, no date (Scrapbook, Robert Altman Archives, University of Michigan Special Collections).

20. Jan Stuart, *The Nashville Chronicles: The Making of Robert Altman's Masterpiece* (Simon & Schuster, 2000), 279.

21. Author's Interview with Alan Rudolph, October 23, 2023.

22. Curiously, the screenplay was published in April 1976, long after the

film's domestic release. The potential benefit of the book for generating interest in watching or rewatching the film was lost.

23. Perri, 11.

24. Robin Wood, "Smart-Ass and Cutie-Pie: Notes Toward the Evaluation of Altman (1975)," in Wood, *Hollywood from Vietnam to Reagan* (Columbia University Press, 1986), 26–45.

25. In some foreign markets, the Myers artwork was combined with a different tagline than those used in the jean- jacket ad. For the Australian release, distributor Cinema International Corporation created a poster with the Myers artwork and, compared to the jean-jacket ad, a much more specific and descriptive tagline: "*Nashville* is Corrupt, Innocent, Beautiful, Vulgar, Sentimental, Shocking, Exuberant, and Fabulous. *Nashville* is about Big People, Little People, Cycle Freaks, and Groupies; Candidates, Crackpots and Lovers; Simple Folk, Crazy Folk and Chock-Full of Music."

26. The Restricted rating is a curious aspect of *Nashville*. As several critics noted, one profanity uttered by Mary contributed to the rating. Altman could have easily replaced the word and been given a PG rating. This would have made the film available to a much larger audience.

27. As Charles Michener describes in his *Newsweek* cover article, "[*Nashville*] is also that rarest thing in contemporary movies—a work of art that promises to be hugely popular." ("Altman's Opryland Epic," *Newsweek*, June 30, 1975, 46).

28. Ray McClain, "Nashville Looks at M*A*S*Hville," *After Dark* (October 1975), 28.

29. Stuart Byron, "First Annual 'Grosses Gloss,'" *Film Comment* (March-April 1976), 31.

30. The dancing microphone poster included, at times, the quote from Pauline Kael: "The funniest epic vision of America ever to reach the screen." This quote could easily have been used as a brand filter to take advantage of the comedy appeal and to build the film's advertising, marketing, and publicity campaigns.

Chapter 5

1. I am including neither images from interviews with *Nashville* actors nor frame grabs from the film. Other images from online sources or from articles (academic or editorial) are also omitted from this analysis. My goal is to focus exclusively on the image selection in the Altman archive.

2. Roland Barthes, "The Third Meaning," *Image-Music-Text* (Hill and Wang, 1977), 52.

3. Barthes, 54.

4. Philip Watts, *Roland Barthes' Cinema* (Oxford University Press, 2016), 51.

5. Marvin Heiferman, "Processed Promises," *Still Life* (Callaway Editions, 1983).

6. Diane Keaton, "Appearances Are Deceptive," *Still Life* (Callaway Editions, 1983), 1–2.

7. Karina Longworth, *Hollywood Frame By Frame: The Unseen Silver Screen in Contact Sheets, 1951–1997* (Princeton Architectural Press, 2014), 9.

8. Quoted in Longworth, 149.

9. Longworth, 9.

10. Jonathan Gray, "Text," in *Keywords for Media Studies*, ed. Laurie Ouellette and Jonathan Gray (NYU Press, 2017), 199.

11. Some of the Pagliuso images are used in background images as part of album covers and song sheets during the film's opening-credits sequence. This complete set of images was reproduced in Pagliuso's *In Plain Sight: The Photographs, 1968–2017* (Damiani, 2018).

12. Another aspect of the wardrobe continuity sheets is information on casting provided at the top of each sheet. For instance, the character of Kenny is initially listed as being played by Michael Burns (who starred in Altman's *That Cold Day in the Park*), whose name is crossed out and replaced by "David Hayward."

13. Note that the current analysis is not of color stills used as part of an in-theater display or at the front entrance of a movie theater. I am focusing solely on the black-and-white stills that are typically part of a review or article.

14. Author's Interview with Robert Altman, April 11, 2000.

15. Stuart, 211.

16. It should be noted that, compared to Joan Tewkesbury's fourth-draft screenplay, Altman considerably expanded the presence of Opal in the final film.

17. The recording studio is also validated by a wardrobe costume continuity shot showing Richard Baskin wearing his outfit from that scene in the contact sheet. The wardrobe shot is labeled as "Recording Studio Musician."

18. Joan Tewkesbury, *Nashville* (Bantam Books, 1976).

19. In an interview (April 25, 2024), Joan Tewkesbury indicated that the scene was designed to show Kelly protecting Barbara Jean from a concert attendee who had started to berate her loudly.

20. Jonathan Gray, *Show Sold Separately: Promos, Spoilers, and Other Media Paratexts* (NYU Press, 2010), 25.

21. Rebecca Baron, "The Idea of Still," *Still Moving: Between Cinema and Photography*, ed. Karen Redrobe and Jean Ma (Duke University Press, 2008), 125.

Bibliography

Abrahams, Steven. "Buying *Nashville*." *Jump Cut* 9 (1975): 6–7.

Altman, Kathryn Reed, and Giulia D'Agnolo Vallan. *Altman*. Abrams, 2014.

Altman, Rick. "24-Track Narrative? Robert Altman's *Nashville*." *Cinemas: Journal of Film Studies* 1, no. 3 (2000): 102–25.

Armstrong, Rick, ed. *Robert Altman Critical Essays*. McFarland & Company, 2011.

Baker, Charles A. "Illusion and Reality in *Nashville*." *Studies in the Humanities* 10, no. 2 (1983): 93–98.

Beck, Jay. "The Democratic Voice: Altman's Sound Aesthetics in the 1970s." *A Companion to Robert Altman*, ed. Adrian Danks, 184–209. Wiley Blackwell, 2015.

Blim, Dan. "'You Don't Belong in Nashville!': Politics, Country Music, and the Reception of Robert Altman's *Nashville*." *Music & Politics* 16, no. 2 (Summer 2022): 1–27.

Bowles, Stephen E. "*Cabaret* and *Nashville*: The Musical as Social Comment." *Journal of Popular Culture* 12 (Winter 1978): 550–56.

Byrne, Connie, and William O. Lopez. "*Nashville*." *Film Quarterly* 29 (Winter 1975–76): 13–25.

Cardullo, Robert. "The Space in the Distance: A Study of Altman's *Nashville*." *Literature/Film Quarterly* 4, no. 4 (Fall 1976): 313–24.

Caso, Frank. *Robert Altman in the American Grain*. Reaktion Books, 2015.

Cook, Bruce. "Patronizing the Nashville Sound." *New Leader*, July 21, 1975: 29.

Corrigan, Timothy. *A Cinema without Walls: Movies and Culture after Vietnam*. Rutgers University Press, 1991.

Danks, Adrian, ed. *A Companion to Robert Altman*. Wiley Blackwell, 2015.

Diller, Barry. *Who Knew*. Simon & Schuster, 2025.

Elsaesser, Thomas. "*Nashville*: Putting on the Show." *Persistence of Vision* 1 (1984): 35–43.

Farber, Stephen. "Let Us Now Praise—Not Overpraise—Robert Altman." *New York Times*, September 29, 1975: 2.1.

Feuer, Jane. "*Nashville*, Altman's Open Surface." *Jump Cut* 10/11 (1976): 31–32.

Fox, Terry Curtis, "*Nashville* Chats." *Chicago Reader*, July 4, 1976: 1–20.

Gans, Herbert J. "*Nashville*: The Film as a Statement about Society." *Social Policy* 6 (November/December 1975): 57–58.

Gilbey, Ryan. *It Don't Worry Me: Nashville, Jaws, Star Wars and Beyond.* Faber and Faber, 2003.

Gross, Larry. "An Interview with Robert Altman on the Set of *Nashville*." *Millimeter* 3 (February 1975): 24–29.

Haskell, Molly. "*Nashville*." *Village Voice*, June 11, 1975.

Hendershot, Heather. *Nashville* (BFI Film Classic). Bloomsbury Publishing, 2025.

Hoberman, J. "NASHVILLE Contra JAWS, or 'The Imagination of Disaster Revisited.'" *The Last Great American Picture Show*, ed. Thomas Elsaesser, Noel King, Alexander Howarth. Amsterdam University Press, 2004.

Horn, Chris. *The Lost Decade: Altman, Coppola, Friedkin and the Hollywood Renaissance Auteur in the 1980s*. Bloomsbury Academic, 2024.

Jacobs, Diane. *Hollywood Renaissance.* A. S. Barnes, 1977.

Jameson, Richard T. "*Nashville*: Writin' It Down Kinda Makes Me Feel Better." *Movietone News*, September 4, 1975: 1–24.

Kael, Pauline. "Coming: *Nashville*." *New Yorker*, March 3, 1975: 79–84.

Karp, Alan. *The Films of Robert Altman*. Scarecrow, 1981.

Kass, Judith M. *Robert Altman: American Innovator*. Popular Library, 1978.

Keyssar, Helene. *Robert Altman's America*. Oxford University Press, 1991.

Klein, Michael. "*Nashville* and the American Dream." *Jump Cut* 9 (1975): 6–7.

Kolker, Robert. *A Cinema of Loneliness: Penn, Stone, Kubrick, Scorsese, Spielberg*, 3rd ed. Oxford University Press, 2000.

Lev, Peter. *American Film of the 70s: Conflicting Visions*. University of Texas Press, 2000.

Levin, Sid. "The Art of the Editor: *Nashville*." *Filmmaker Newsletter* 8, no. 10 (1975): 29–33.

Lewin, Alex. "It Happened in Nashville." *Premiere* 13, no. 11 (July 2000): 88–95, 101–2, 20.

Lippy, Tod. "Writing *Nashville*: A Talk with Joan Tewkesbury." *Scenario* 1 (Winter 1995): 105–9, 205.

Macklin, Anthony F. "*Nashville*: America's Voices." *Film Heritage* 11, no. 1 (1975): 6–10.

Magee, Gayle Sherwood. *Robert Altman's Soundtracks*. Oxford University Press, 2014.

McClain, Ray. "Nashville Looks at M*A*S*Hville." *After Dark*, October 1975.

McGilligan, Patrick. *Robert Altman: Jumping Off the Cliff*. St. Martin's Press, 1989.

Michener, Charles, and Martin Kasindorf. "Altman's Opryland Epic." *Newsweek*, June 30, 1975: 46–50.

Minett, Mark. *Robert Altman and the Elaboration of Hollywood Storytelling*. Oxford University Press, 2021.

Monaco, James. *American Film Now*. New American Library, 1979.

Ness, Richard. "'Doing Some Replacin'': Gender, Genre and the Subversion of Dominant Ideology in the Music Scene." *Robert Altman Critical Essays*, ed. Rick Armstrong. McFarland and Company, 2011.

Niemi, Robert. *The Cinema of Robert Altman: Hollywood Maverick*. Wallflower Press, 2016.

Pagliuso, Jean. *In Plain Sight: The Photographs, 1968–2017*. Grafiche Damiani, 2018.

Perri, Dan. *Hollywood Titles Designer: A Life in Film*. Finchley Central Films, 2020.

Plecki, Gerard. *Robert Altman*. Twayne, 1985.

Pye, Michael, and Linda Myles. *The Movie Brats: How the Film Generation Took Over Hollywood*. Holt, Rinehart & Winston, 1979.

Ridley, Jim. "Look Back in Anger." *Nashville Scene*, November 9, 1995.

Rollin, Roger B. "Robert Altman's *Nashville*: Popular Film and the American Character." *South Atlantic Bulletin* 42 (November 1977): 41–50.

Russell, Catherine. "*Nashville*: The Show Must Explode." *Narrative Mortality: Death, Closure, and New Wave Cinemas*. University of Minnesota Press, 1995: 192–208.

Schreger, Charles. "Altman, Dolby, and the Second Sound Revolution." *Film Sound: Theory and Practice*, ed. Elisabeth Weis and John Belton. Columbia University Press, 1985.

Self, Robert. "Invention and Death: The Commodities of Media in Robert Altman's *Nashville*." *Journal of Popular Film* 5 (1976).

Self, Robert. *Robert Altman's Subliminal Reality*. University of Minnesota Press, 2002.

Sterritt, David, ed. *Robert Altman: Interviews*. University of Mississippi Press, 2000.

Sterritt, David. "Robert Altman: Documentaries, Dreamscapes and Dialogic Cinema." *When the Movies Mattered: The New Hollywood Revisited*, ed. Jon Lewis and Jonathan Kirschner, 69–85. Cornell University Press, 2019.

Stuart, Jan. *The Nashville Chronicles: The Making of Robert Altman's Masterpiece*. Simon & Schuster, 2000.

Tewkesbury, Joan. *Nashville* (Original Screenplay). Bantam Books, 1976.
Thompson, David. *Altman on Altman*. Faber and Faber, 2006.
Tsiolkas, Christos. "Altman: The Artist in Middle Age" *A Companion to Robert Altman*, ed. Adrian Danks. 390–400. Wiley Blackwell, 2015.
Viertel, Jack, and David Walker. "The Long Road to *Nashville*." *New York Times*, June 13, 1975: 52–58.
Vonnegut, Kurt, Jr. "*Nashville*: A Shadow Play of What We Have Become and Where We Might Look for Wisdom." *Vogue*, June 1975: 103.
Weintraub, Jerry, and Rich Cohen. *When I Stop Talking, You'll Know I'm Dead*. Twelve, 2010.
Wexman, Virginia Wright. "The Rhetoric of Cinematic Improvisation." *Cinema Journal* 20, no. 1 (Fall 1980): 29–41.
Wexman, Virginia Wright. "*Nashville*: Second City Performance Comes to Hollywood." *A Companion to Robert Altman*, ed. Adrian Danks, 369–89. Wiley Blackwell, 2015.
Wicker, Tom. "*Nashville*: Dark Perceptions in a Country Music Comedy." *New York Times*, June 15, 1975: 2.1, 2.17.
Wood, Robin. "Smart-Ass and Cutie-Pie: Notes Toward the Evaluation of Altman (1975)" *Hollywood from Vietnam to Reagan*. Columbia University Press, 1986: 26–45.
Wyatt, Justin. "Economic Constraints/Economic Opportunities: Robert Altman as Auteur." *Velvet Light Trap* 38 (Fall 1996): 52–67.
Wyatt, Justin, "Weighing the Transgressive Star Body of Shelley Duvall," in *Sex & Money: Feminism and Political Economy in the Media*, eds. Eileen R. Meehan and Ellen Riordan. 147–63. University of Minnesota Press, 2002.
Yacowar, Maurice. "Actors as Conventions in the Films of Robert Altman." *Cinema Journal* 20 (Fall 1980): 14–28.
Yates, John. "Smart Man's Burden: *Nashville, A Face in the Crowd* and Popular Culture." *Journal of Popular Film* 5, no. 1 (1976): 19–28.
Zuckoff, Mitchell. *Robert Altman: The Oral Biography*. Alfred A. Knopf, 2009.

Index